Francis
de
Sales

Finding God
wherever
You Are

Francis de Sales

Finding God
wherever
You Are

*selected
spiritual writings*

introduced and edited by
Joseph F. Power
Oblate of Saint Francis de Sales

New City Press

Published in the United States by New City Press
86 Mayflower Avenue, New Rochelle, New York 10801
©1993 New City Press

Library of Congress Cataloging-in-Publication Data:

Francis, de Sales, Saint, 1567-1622.
    Finding God wherever you are : selected spiritual writings /
Francis de Sales ; introduced and edited by Joseph F. Power.

    ISBN 1-56548-021-X ; $8.95
    1. Spiritual life--Catholic authors--Early works to 1800.
I. Power, Joseph F.   II. Title.
BX2349.F693   1993
248.4'82--dc20   92-44973

Printed in the United States of America

Contents

In Life

Toward the Integration of Life and Prayer

Introduction

Deep within, every human being is searching: there is the search of those who, consciously or not seek God, and there is the search of those who, having "found" God in some degree of faith, seek for ways to deepen their contact with the divine in prayer and to live in relationship with God. This book is intended as a help in this second search for concrete ways to respond to God, the search for a "spirituality."

Over the centuries Christian preachers and spiritual writers have proposed many ways to respond to the God revealed in Jesus and his gospel. Historically most of the classic Christian spiritualities are products of a life somewhat removed from ordinary life "in the world," and the usual relationships of family, work and politics, and so tend to assume as much withdrawal or solitude as possible. This spirituality "of the desert" or monastic spirituality still speaks to many today; in fact in its various adaptations it continues to exert such a powerful influence that some think it is the only model: to respond more fully to God I must follow Jesus into the desert, spend hours in quiet prayer, do some kind of fasting, get away on a silent retreat as often as possible, and know that in all this I am embarking on a journey "alone with the alone."

As powerfully attractive as the model is, the difficulties of living it in anything but a monastic or solitary setting are evident. How can one find that kind of solitude or that kind of time away when one is raising a family or pursuing a career in business, building, the arts or politics? And if one feels called to the latter in faith, as a matter of vocation, does it mean that one is not called to a deeper spirituality, or at least not now? Or does it mean that God is indeed asking me to do the impossible in my present situation? Or is there another model?

Almost four hundred years ago Francis de Sales (1567-1622) clearly and consciously thought and taught that there are many other models of spirituality, other forms of "devotion" than the monastic or religious-life model. He sought to outline a way people could live God's love fully, with the alacrity and intensity that he called "devotion" within families, in the workplace, even—to use modern equivalents of what he said—in the military or in government. He personally helped such people find ways of living this life through personal spiritual direction and letters, and eventually wrote a book for them, an *Introduction to the Devout Life*. He also published what has been called a sequel, a *Treatise on the Love of God*, elaborating the inner workings of that love for God as it grows in human hearts.

The selections contained in this anthology are drawn from these letters and books. The arrangement, the headings, and the rest of this introduction are intended to help twentieth-century searchers "hear" a seventeenth-century writer—to hear him in a way that offers direction and encouragement in their own search for ways of responding to God.

Some readers may not need these helps, and may well go directly to the texts, but the fact remains that we are dealing with writings as old as Shakespeare's, and translations of French writings at that. And these writings, coming from a world quite different from our own, can be understood properly only in that larger historical and social context.

There is, to be sure, no lack of contemporary writers who propose ways of responding to God in the very different conditions of today's world. Since they do not need to be translated from another time or language, some will prefer to read them. At the same time, there is an enrichment to be gained through contact with classic spiritual writings. Whatever the effort required, there is an advantage in reading what not only has survived the passage of centuries, but what has continued to provide spiritual nourishment to countless readers of various eras, cultures, and walks of life. Their testimony has its own weight, as does the approbation of the Roman Catholic Church which has long since declared that Francis de Sales lived a remarkably Christian life—that he is a saint (1665), and that he taught that life well, that he is a doctor or teacher of the whole Church (1877).

In any case to introduce the texts themselves I propose to say something about the several worlds in which Francis lived, always with an eye to understanding his life and writings. Then, after listing a few characteristics of his spirituality, I will suggest ways in which that spirituality needs to be completed and inserted in the "worlds" of today.

Francis de Sales' Worlds

From several points of view, Francis de Sales occupied a space and time between two worlds, in each of which he was able to be at home, and both of which he was able to integrate within himself. Geographically he lived most of his life in his native Savoy, for centuries an independent duchy which spanned the Alps and included parts of what is now France and Italy. After early education in Savoy, Francis went first to Paris to study the humanities and philosophy, and then to Padua to study law. He thus had many direct and extended experiences of the two cultures which converged in Savoy, as well as of the Church as it existed in either.

Historically Francis lived in a time of enormous cultural and religious transition, a transition from the last breath of the medieval worldview and the clear awakenings of the modern, more specifically in that period between the Renaissance and the Enlightenment that some call the Baroque. In terms of Church history he lived in the period of Roman Catholic revival which had begun in sixteenth-century Italy and Spain, but which, in the heart of Europe where Francis lived, had been enormously affected by the Protestant Reformation. In fact Francis grew up in a staunchly Catholic family in the shadow of Calvin's Geneva; though he eventually bore the title of Prince and Bishop of Geneva, he was able to visit the city only incognito and at some risk. By his loyalty to the "ancient Church," its institutions and teachers, he had one foot in the medieval period. At the same time the other foot was clearly in the modern, as is evidenced by his writing an emerging modern French, by his intuitive psychological insight, and by his anticipation of modern spirituality, as will be seen shortly.

Socially Francis moved easily in many different worlds of his time, notably in two worlds which were increasingly differentiated in his day, the secular and the ecclesiastical. By virtue not only of his formal education but also of his sustained interest in literature, science, diplomacy and civility, Francis was a humanist. At the same time he was, at first by desire and then in fact "of the Church," an expression which in his day meant a cleric, but which can express a deeper belonging which stemmed from his baptism. "This country [Savoy] is my homeland according to my natural birth; according to my spiritual re-birth, my homeland is the Church."[1] That simply did he join the two in himself, differentiating but integrating the two worlds: human and Christian.

In other respects as well, Francis joined disparate worlds in himself,

---

1. Letter of December 16, 1619 to Angelique Arnauld. *Oeuvres de Saint François de Sales, Edition complète*, 27 vols. (Annecy: J. Niérat *et al.*, 1892-1964), XIX, 74. This Annecy edition will be cited hereafter as *Oeuvres*, followed by the volume and page numbers.

the active and contemplative, lay and religious, indeed the human and the divine, but, since these integrations pertain directly to his spirituality, they will be seen later, under that heading.

Against this very general geographical, historical, social and religious background, I propose to leave the telling of Francis' life story to others[1] and simply to highlight a few facets of it which help explain how he was prepared to live and write as he did.

Education. Francis de Sales was ordained a priest at the age of twenty-five and bishop nine years later without ever having been in a seminary. From an early age he knew he wanted to be a priest, but he kept that desire a secret all through the years of his education, confiding it only to his cousin Louis de Sales, to his spiritual director, and at some point to his mother. As a result, at Paris Francis received a thoroughly "lay" education typical for the nobility of his era, and at Padua he studied both civil and canon law as all prospective lawyers did. He did all this, as he said later, "to please my father," while at the same time, both in Paris and Padua, he studied theology "to please myself." Without questioning Francis' spontaneous interest in theology, one may suppose that he knew such studies were necessary for his goal of ordained ministry. Even more importantly, all through this time he was growing spiritually, through spiritual direction and reading, prayer and religious exercises, and not without crises, both psychological and theological in nature.[2]

Even after receiving his degree in law with great acclaim, Francis was reluctant to ask his aging father's permission to become a priest. He was admitted to the bar in the Savoyard capital of Chambery, but declined not only an arranged marriage but also the offer of a seat in the Senate of Savoy. Finally, at the instigation of his cousin Louis and others, letters arrived from Rome naming Francis Provost of the Cathedral Chapter, a position second to the bishop. With this concession to his father's expectation for an eldest son in hand, Francis approached him and received a magnanimous blessing. Within eight months, he had also received minor orders, diaconate and priesthood, more than satisfying all the requirements.

Is it any wonder, then, that Francis de Sales as priest and bishop could minister so effectively to all classes of people, that in particular, he could

---

1. For example, Michael de la Bedoyere, *François de Sales* (New York: Harper, 1960), or Andre Ravier, S.J., *Francis de Sales, Sage and Saint*, tr. Joseph D. Bowler, O.S.F.S. (San Francisco: Ignatius, 1988).

2. On the two related crises of Francis' youth, see Ravier, *Sage and Saint*, pp. 29-34 and 37-39.

understand the situation and direct the hearts of lay people? Or that he would write his *Introduction to the Devout Life* for them and for all who have "to lead an ordinary life to all outward appearances"?[1] He knew from experience what it meant to live an ordinary life while inwardly growing in God's love and nurturing God's inspirations.

Friends. Francis de Sales had a great personal capacity and a profound appreciation for friendship, seeing both human and divine friendship as that for which we are made.

To all his friendships he brought a heart gifted for love, and by them all—in varying degrees, to be sure—he was enriched and his spirituality was shaped. Whether it was his friendship with Pernette Boutey, a widow with a small business in a village of his diocese, or his friendship with King Henry IV of France, Francis grew through his friendships.[2]

Though he derived much from many, for example, the many spiritual persons he met during a 1602 stay in Paris, he gained even more from his long-term spiritual direction relationships, and uniquely from that with Jane Frances de Chantal.[3] She was a young widow with four small children and an intense desire to give herself totally to God. From their first meeting in 1604, theirs was a graced relationship, and it became one of the great spiritual friendships in Christian history. Shortly after they met, Francis agreed to be her spiritual director; for him, though, spiritual direction was never a one-way street, and when it grew in depth it tended to become a more and more mutual relationship, a true friendship, a gracefilled gift to himself as well as to the other.

Some have exaggerated the influence of his more famous spiritual friends to the point of depicting Francis as the attentive novice doing his studies in the Paris circle, or as a faithful reporter recording the experience of Jane de Chantal in the *Treatise on the Love of God*. In reality he brought much to these encounters, and the exchange was mutual; so much so in the latter case that it is pointless to ask who influenced whom the most.[4]

---

1. *Introduction to the Devout Life*, Preface, tr. Armind Nazareth, Antony Mookenthottam and Antony Kolencherry, Missionaries of St. Francis de Sales (Bangalore: SFS Publications, 1990), p. 2. This work will be cited as *Introduction*, followed by indication of the part and chapter, and, if this translation is used, SFS ed., and page number.
2. Cf. Ravier, *Sage and Saint*, pp. 94 and 136f.
3. See Wendy Wright, *Bond of Perfection* (New York/Mahwah: Paulist Press, 1985), or Ravier, pp. 127ff.
4. "It is useless to ask which of the two, St. Francis de Sales or Saint Chantal, was the teacher of the other. . . . What reasonable person would not agree that the

What is essential is to see that the same Holy Spirit, working primarily in and through Francis' unique heart and personality, was also inspiring and enriching his spirituality through his relationships with friends, and that, as a result, his life and personality can be understood only in that relational context. This also explains the influence he had on others, both during his lifetime and beyond, a powerful but never over-powering influence which passed from person to person, directly or through his writing. His ability to listen gave him the ability and the language to speak and write in a way that touched hearts. "Say what you will," he wrote, "lips speak but to ears; heart speaks to heart."[1] His heart was neither a sponge drawing only from those around him, nor a precious stone, gifted but impervious to others' gifts. It was rather a constantly pulsating heart-center which never ceased drawing in and giving forth God's love.[2] It was a heart gifted through others, and a heart gifted to share with others.

Ministry. Francis' sense of his own vocation to serve God as an ordained minister serving God's people, a sense which grew in clarity and strength from his earliest years, gave a consistent direction to his entire life. One cannot understand him or his spirituality without appreciating that pastoral focus. Alluding to his consecration as bishop, Francis once recounted to his friend Jane a sermon he had given the day before: "I said that it is ten years since I was consecrated, that is, since God took me from myself to take me to himself and give me to his people, which is to say, since God converted me from what I was so that I might be for them."[3]

So strong was this sense of total consecration that we can say that all his activities were done for God and for the spiritual well-being of the people. This became the central criterion he used in deciding how to spend his time and energies. As priest and even more so as bishop, the demands on his time were great. "I don't think there is a bishop for a hundred miles around who has such an entangled mass of things to do as I have."[4]

---

teacher became the irreplaceable friend in a dialogue ... where they built and developed in common a theology and a spirituality of union in diversity, or of 'unidiversity' as the *Treatise* says?" Hélène Bordes, "La Mère de Chantal, Maîtresse d'oraison," XVIIᵉ Siecle, No. 144 (July-December, 1984), 211f.

1. Letter to André Fremyot, October 5, 1604, *Oeuvres* XII, 321.
2. For the image see *The Love of God, a Treatise* by Saint Francis de Sales, tr. Vincent Kerns, M.S.F.S. (Westminster, Md.: Newman, 1962), p. 212. This work will be abbreviated as *Treatise*, followed by indication of book and chapter, in this case, V, 12.
3. Letter to Jane de Chantal, December 9, 1612, *Oeuvres* XV, 312f.
4. Letter to Pierre de Villars, *cir.* February 15, 1609, *Oeuvres* XIV, 125.

Administering and reforming his diocese took much of his time, but priority was given to preaching, celebrating the sacraments, and teaching catechism personally to children.

His pastoral ministry also included the previously mentioned spiritual direction in person and by letter of people in his diocese and beyond. His direction of Jane de Chantal led to his being co-founder with her of the Visitation of Holy Mary. From the beginning Francis saw this community as another way of meeting the spiritual needs of people, and not only those of the women who joined it: the Visitation was to be a community of prayer, but radiating holiness to the whole Church.[1]

It was this same pastoral care that accounts for all of Francis' writings, most of which derived from his direct response to people's needs, without necessarily being intended for publication. His missionary work as a priest endeavoring to win back to the Catholic faith the Calvinists of the Chablais region prompted him to write short tracts or memoranda "on the Church" and "on the norms of faith," which were posthumously published as *The Catholic Controversy*. In the same context he himself published a *Defense of the Standard of the Cross* as a direct retort to Calvinist attacks on Catholic practice.

The first edition of the *Introduction to the Devout Life* grew out of memoranda on the spiritual life written for individuals, which he was soon persuaded to publish. Its immediate success was so great that Francis saw it as a way of helping more and more people; he expanded it into the form which has become a religious best seller of all time, constantly republished, translated and adapted.

The more than two thousand letters that have come down to us are an obvious record of his pastoral ministry, from administration to spiritual direction, and the four volumes of sermons testify to what he saw as the focus of his ministry as bishop. The *Spiritual Conferences* are the transcription of familiar instructions and responses he gave to the first members of the Visitation community and were eventually published by them.

One might wonder about the *Treatise on the Love of God*, which by its title and early sections seems to be a more theoretical work, designed to think through the intricacies of theology and prayer. Granted that it originated in Francis' own desire to tell the story of God's love, and not

---

1. See André Ravier, in *Saint François de Sales, Oeuvres* (Paris: Gallimard, 1969), pp. xlvi-xlvii.

from any specific pastoral need, still as it developed and took shape it became a book people were waiting for, a follow-up to the *Introduction*, and every bit as "practical" a book, that is, intended to guide the practice of Christian life and prayer.

For Francis the mystical life is life—everyday life, with events foreseen and unforeseeable, with its sufferings and its joys, its friendships and its separations, its worries and its consolations—natural life but totally penetrated, "soaked through and through" to use his expression, by and in the will of God. . . .

That is how, it seems to us, one must understand the *Treatise on the Love of God*. It is a book about life, about the life of a Christian who wants to sound the depths of faith, but within the actual concrete situations in which that Christian exists in each moment. . . . This *Treatise on the Love of God* is not a book to be used only by contemplatives, no more than it is a book only for activists; the love of God it talks about is situated beyond contemplation as well as beyond activity; it is at the source of both contemplation and action; it is the life of the complete Christian, a life full of love.[1]

This portrait of Francis' major work bears an unmistakable resemblance to the author's own active-contemplative life; it shows that even this apparently theoretical work flowed straight from his heart and was inspired by his pastoral care for other hearts seeking the fullness of love in their circumstances and everyday life. It follows that what we have in his writings is a "mysticism in action," a spirituality encompassing the highest forms of prayer yet lived in a very active life. That is important to know, both for understanding Francis de Sales and for relating his spirituality to busy lives today.

Characteristics of His Spirituality

My intent here is neither to summarize nor to select highlights of Salesian[2] spirituality. Either aim might imply that a reading of Francis

---

1. *Ibid.* , pp. lxxxi-lxxxii.

2. The word "Salesian" derives, of course, from Francis' family name; as applied to spirituality it may be understood as designating the unique spiritual doctrine

himself is optional, and that would defeat the purpose of this book. No, the intent here is to describe some characteristics of Salesian spirituality which will prepare the reader to approach the texts with a clearer idea of their originality and modernity. These characteristics are not always obvious, but by alerting the reader to them in advance, I hope to facilitate the appreciation of the texts and their content.

Salesian Spirituality Starts from the Heart and Grows Outward

This characteristic is consciously and explicitly stated by Francis himself:

As for myself, Philothea, I could never approve the method of those who begin by the exterior such as the bearing, the dress or the hair in order to reform a person. On the contrary, it seems to me that we should begin by the interior: "Convert yourself to me, says God, with your whole heart" (Jl 2:12). "My child, give me your heart" (Prv 23:26). As the heart is the source of actions, they are such as the heart is. The divine spouse inviting us says: "Place me as a seal on your heart, as a seal on your arm" (Sg 8:6). Yes, indeed, those who have Jesus Christ in their hearts will have him soon after in all their exterior actions.

I wish, therefore, dear Philothea, to engrave and inscribe on your heart, before everything else, this holy and sacred maxim: Live Jesus! After that, I am sure that your life which comes from your heart . . . will produce all its actions which are its fruits inscribed and engraved with the same word of salvation. Just as the gentle Jesus will live in your heart, he will live also in your conduct and appear in your eyes, in your mouth, in your hands, even in your hair. Then you could say reverently following St. Paul "I live now, not I, but Christ lives in me" (Gal 2:20). In short, to win a person's heart is to win the whole person.[1]

---

emanating from both Francis and Jane de Chantal, from their friendship and mutual sharing. See *Francis de Sales, Jane de Chantal, Letters of Spiritual Direction*, tr. Peronne Marie Thibert, V.H.M., selected and introduced by Wendy M. Wright and Joseph F. Power, O.S.F.S. (New York/Mahwah: Paulist Press, 1988), Introduction, especially pp. 11-13 and 70ff. The word is also used of the Salesians of Don Bosco, a religious order whose original title was "Society of St. Francis de Sales."

1. *Introduction* III, 23; SFS ed., pp. 181f. This passage, and the entire *Introduction*, is addressed to "Philothea," a fictional name, feminine in form, meaning "one

Ironically this passage introduced a chapter on exterior mortification, and continues with the instruction the heart needs "to form its exterior bearing and conduct." That context makes clear from the start that, while this spirituality starts with the interior, it does not remain within, but gradually, "organically" as the accompanying imagery suggests, grows into observable behavior, all the while remaining marked by its inner source.

The starting point within is called the "heart." Lest the understanding of that image be shaped by the connotations attached to that word in current speech or in sentimental piety, it is essential to know what Francis meant by it.

> But let us be very careful to give to the word heart its Salesian meaning: the heart designates here, as in the Bible, that which is most profound, most inalienable, most personal, most divine in us; it is that mysterious center where each encounters God, acquiesces to his appeals or refuses to do so.[1]

Salesian spirituality starts, then, from the deepest core of a person, one's heart-center, where intellect and will, reason and affections, "head and heart" are seen as one, prior to differentiations that may be legitimate and even necessary. For Francis this is a matter as much of theology as of psychology. It follows from the pouring forth of God's love "into our hearts," as St. Paul says, or from the indwelling of the Holy Spirit in our heart of hearts, which Francis also calls the "supreme point of the soul."[2] It is from that point that all "spiritual life" flows, and from there that all the rest derives meaning and value.

To this point the interiority of Salesian spirituality is not unlike that of the New Testament, or of other efforts to overcome a recurring emphasis

---

who loves God." When Francis heard that some men were put off from reading the book by this address, he criticized their logic, yet nevertheless addressed his *Treatise* to "Theotimus," a masculine name meaning the same thing (*Treatise*, Preface). In some languages these names have been used as short titles for the respective books.

1. Ravier, *Sage and Saint*, p. 146. The biblical notion of heart is clearly indicated in the notes of the New Jerusalem Bible (New York: Doubleday, 1985) beginning with the note on Eph 1:18.

2. Cf. Rom 5:5, Gal 4:6. Francis' imagery of the different "parts of the soul" (*Treatise* I, 11, 12) occurs frequently, especially to differentiate the "supreme, or highest, or fine point" of the human spirit. In different imagery, it is roughly synonymous with the "heart of hearts." See A. Ravier in *Saint François de Sales*, *Oeuvres*, p. ci.

on externals in the Christian religion, but it has some consequences that are characteristically Salesian.

1. Because it is a spirituality first and foremost of the heart, Salesian spirituality can be lived in any circumstances or life-style, and it will fit in and improve the circumstances of that life. In this sense it is a "spirituality for all," able to grow from within and adapt itself to any life-style, from that of the busiest business person to that of a contemplative in a monastery. Spiritualities which are built on a particular form of prayer, or around a particular ministry or life-style, by definition cannot have the flexibility of one built on the heart.

2. Because the meaning and value of our actions come from within, they cannot be evaluated from the outside nor according to their seeming importance. Besides, "important tasks lie seldom in our path; but all day long there are little things we can do so well, if we do them with all our love."[1] Or again, "To serve [God] according to his liking, we must take great care to serve him well in great and lofty matters as well as in the little and the lowly. In fact, we can equally delight his heart both by the one and the other."[2]

Francis' "indifference" to great works, indeed his preference for littleness in works, virtues, life-style, etc., can be misunderstood as though he failed to appreciate the inner greatness of human actions and aspirations. Actually his attitude is partly a consequence of his practical preference for what is at hand over what one might dream about doing some day. The omnipresence of little tasks to be accomplished and little virtues to be practiced is their first advantage. Secondly these everyday opportunities are so ordinary as not to attract attention and hence can be responded to "in secret" as the gospel says (Mt 6:4ff), with less risk of hypocrisy or pride.

But underlying these practical and psychological factors lies Francis' conviction that what gives value and importance to actions, great and small, is the heart from which they flow and the love which expresses itself in them.

> That saint, with his draught of cold water for the thirsty traveler—little enough, it seems, his gesture; but so pure his intention, so perfect the kindness, the love, which he puts into

---

1. *Treatise* XII, 6.
2. *Introduction* III, 35; SFS ed., p. 214.

what he is doing, that his simple offering becomes a spring of living water to bring him everlasting life.[1]

3. But the hidden life of the heart must be fostered and cultivated; it is not enough to have begun with a conversion of heart once in the past. The life of the heart must constantly be nourished by prayer—some dedicated prayer time daily as well as frequent moments of turning toward God in the midst of activity; and it must find outward expression in living from the heart in God's presence. It is so easy to get caught up in the world around and even the world within (thoughts, emotions, hurts, etc.) that a constantly renewed effort is needed to keep in touch—or rather to keep getting back in touch—with one's heart-center. Thus the key question that is asked in an annual review of life in the *Introduction* is, "how's your heart?" in relation to God, to yourself, your neighbor, etc.[2] Francis trusts, in effect, that "as the heart is the source of actions, they are such as the heart is."[3]

Salesian Spirituality is Relational Spirituality

Francis is very conscious that the heart-center of the Christians for whom he was writing existed in relationships, not only with God, but with many other people who were part of their lives. Monastic spirituality, based on a premise of "flight from the world," taught that solitude and silence were indispensable means to achieving the goal of being "alone with the alone," and often implied that other relationships were either inimical or incidental to one's personal spiritual journey. Even living in community a monk (from *monos*, meaning one, alone) had but one key relationship, that with the abbot, who in that role spoke for God.

By contrast Francis came to see, in his own experience as well as in that of others, that certain relationships were very much part of the way God works in human hearts, and that for Christians who are called to live "in the world" all relationships are part of their journey to God, and need to be thought of as such. Thus in the *Introduction* he spoke not only of prayer, sacraments and the virtues, but of friendship, marriage, leisure, social gatherings and of work, on the latter suggesting ways of "managing our affairs with great care but without eagerness or anxiety."[4] It has been

---

1. *Treatise* XII, 6, with reference to Mt 10:42.
2. *Introduction* V.
3. *Introduction* III, 23; SFS ed., p. 181.
4. *Introduction* III, 10; SFS ed., p. 143.

noted that the second and final editions of the *Introduction* gave increased priority and space to the "relational virtues."[1] His letters of spiritual direction insist again and again that one's life situation and relationships are integral to one's relationship with God, and cannot be ignored or neglected in the name of the latter.[2]

The whole range of spiritual friendships which Francis both experienced and wrote about also bear out the relational quality of his spirituality. It raised a question which monastic spirituality didn't have to address, namely how one can love God "with all one's heart, mind and strength" and still love one's spouse, children, friends totally and unreservedly; and what if these loves seem more real than one's love for God? Francis responded to this question in the *Treatise* by recognizing in everyday human experience different kinds of love which are total and yet compatible, for example, the love of a woman for her child and for her husband.[3] In reference to human love for God, he wrote:

> God's love is very willing that we have other loves, and often we can scarcely discern which is the principal love of our heart. . . . It often happens that our heart multiplies much more its acts of affection toward creatures than those toward the Creator. Still holy love does not stop being more excellent than other loves as events make clear when the creature is opposed to the Creator, for then we take the side of holy love and submit to it all our other affections.[4]

The very fact that Francis dealt with such issues both personally and in direction of others shows the intimate connection between love of God and love of others in his spirituality. They are two facets of one love which grows or diminishes in one heart. "It is not that one glimpses God despite the persons around one but that one finds God precisely through and with those persons."[5] Many positive implications of this insight remain to be explored.

---

1. Ruth Murphy, *Saint François de Sales et la civilité chrétienne* (Paris: Nizet, 1964), pp. 177f.
2. Cf. *Letters of Spiritual Direction*, pp. 104, 109f, 112, 167, 179.
3. *Treatise* X, 7.
4. *Ibid.*, my translation.
5. *Letters of Spiritual Direction*, Introduction, p. 46. For indications of how this insight might apply to family life, see Wendy M. Wright, *Sacred Dwelling, a Spirituality of Family Life* (New York: Crossroads, 1990).

In the Midst of Movement Salesian Spirituality Finds Peace

To speak of relationship is to speak of change; the give and take, the ups and downs, the known and unknown in any relationship means that it is never static, but keeps changing, growing or waning, and can never be taken for granted. Likewise to have spoken of a spirituality coming from a hidden heart-center and tending to express itself in action is to have spoken of vital growth and movement, a constant interplay between interior and exterior.

In his *Treatise on the Love of God* Francis de Sales endeavored to express his spirituality entirely in terms of love, which meant distinguishing the many different forms love takes on. Expressed in his original and somewhat technical vocabulary, they usually came in pairs: love of complacence or of benevolence, affective and effective love, love of conformity and love of submission, with each being necessary in turn, alternating and complementing the other.

This is because Francis saw love in all its forms as movement or activity.[1] Prior to other distinctions, love of complacence and benevolence are compared to breathing in and breathing out, or to a heart constantly expanding and contracting. The distinction between affective love (prayer in all its forms) and effective love (concrete expressions of love in life and activities) also implies a complementary and alternating relationship. Both are necessary; they reinforce one another.

The difference between love of conformity and love of submission corresponds to a necessary distinction Francis saw in the ways God's will is made known to us, either through commandments, counsels and inspirations (the "signified will of God") or through events, which, "once they have happened, show us that God has willed" or at least permitted them to happen.[2] This distinction in turn sets up a dynamic conception in which Christian life is seen as "living between the one will of God and the other,"[3] that is, following God's directives as best one can know them and accepting what is or what happens beyond our control as somehow part of God's loving plan or providence.

---

1. "Since it is indisputable that as long as we are in this world, divine love is a movement, or at least an active disposition tending to movement, even when it has arrived at simple union it does not cease acting—however imperceptibly—in order more and more to deepen and complete the union." *Treatise* VII, 1; my translation.

2. *Treatise* IX, 1. Cf. *Ibid.* IX, 7 and 8 for Francis' discussion of how God "permits" evil and suffering to exist in the world.

3. *Ibid.* IX, 7. See *Letters of Spiritual Direction*, Introduction, pp. 40-43.

In these and other ways Francis de Sales' conception of Christian life is dynamic, filled with movement, change and tension—all of which is typical of Baroque culture and style. At the same time his spirit is one of peace, of balance and equilibrium, and his spirituality proves to be peace-producing. A paradox? Perhaps, but it should be noted that his notion of peace is itself dynamic.

The most advanced union with God in prayer is not static but rather that of a free and gentle movement of the heart, or like an infant at its mother's breast.[1] His notion of Christian life was a balance of prayer and activity, a smooth alternation of the roles of Martha and Mary.[2] His ideal of a person in tune with God's will was one who was equally disposed to follow the signified will with determination and gracefully to accept the will of God's good pleasure contained in the outcome, thus living peacefully "between the one will of God and the other"—in a space which at first might be experienced as tension-filled or even contradictory, but which comes to be embraced by living each moment in God's presence and therefore in peace.

In other words, the peace that Francis' spirituality offers is not an alternative to activity but peace in the midst of activity, and activity in the midst of peace: "The one who can preserve gentleness in the midst of sorrows and sufferings and peace in the midst of the multiplicity and busyness of affairs—that person is almost perfect."[3]

Salesian Spirituality Today

These three characteristics, namely, to grow from the heart outward, to embrace one's relationships and work, and to foster inner peace in the midst of activity and busyness, point both to the uniqueness of Salesian spirituality and to its modernity. To the extent that contemporary culture tends to value personal interiority and authenticity, to appreciate relationships and social contexts, and to seek peace of heart—to that extent this seventeenth-century spirituality will appear surprisingly modern.

At the same time it is important to point out some modern assumptions

1. *Treatise* VI, 9 and VII, 1.
2. Letter to Jane de Chantal, August 16, 1607. *Oeuvres* XIII, 309-10.
3. Letter to Mere de Brechard, July 22, 1616. *Oeuvres* XVII, 260.

and awarenesses which are not present in Francis' writings, because in some major areas the social and religious conditions of his time made implausible if not impossible what the Second Vatican Council has made both possible and central for Catholics, and what many Christians consider necessary to any spirituality today.

A liturgical spirituality, in the sense of a way of Christian living consciously drawn from and nourished by direct participation in the holy mysteries, was hardly a possibility in Francis' day. The liturgical language itself, and even more, the liturgical rites long since removed from the changing mentality of ordinary people, resulted in a gap between them. Granted that the sublime significance and centrality of the eucharist, the "sun of the spiritual exercises," the "center of the Christian religion, the heart of devotion," was recognized, the way of participating in it was purely a matter of "interior acts," which could be made by the faithful, as it were, in parallel to what the priest was doing at the altar. In fact, if one could not be present at Mass, the same acts could be made at home.[1] Apart from moments like the reception of communion, which itself was much less frequent in those days, Salesian interiority was out of tangible contact with its sacramental source.

Recognizing the limitations imposed on Salesian spirituality by the historical conditions of its origins need not lead to abandoning it. It does point out the need to supplement the historical spirituality with the liturgical realities and spirituality that are so available today. It may be that Salesian interiority, when brought into vital contact with an accessible liturgy, will provide needed heart and soul for faith-filled celebrations.

Something very similar can be said about the role of scripture in Salesian spirituality. Francis consistently urged his directees to focus their prayer on the life, passion and death of Jesus, and to use various meditation books for that purpose. He could not refer them to the New Testament texts themselves, simply because no approved Catholic translation existed at that time. Today the way is open to pray directly from the text of the entire Bible, to draw the "reflections" for meditation from the scriptural words themselves.

Finally the post-Vatican II era has led to an awareness that action for change in the structures of society is an essential and integral part of the Christian gospel and hence of a fully Christian spirituality. The need is increasingly felt for spiritualities which by their own inner logic lead to

1. *Introduction* II, 14.

making a difference for peace and justice in the contemporary world. To look for such a spirituality in Francis de Sales would be both futile and unfair. As a person of his time, he took society and its institutions pretty much as a given. As a person trained in law, he certainly struggled for justice and fairness, but generally within the framework of existing laws and institutions, without imagining that these might be notably changed. Such an awareness would have to wait another two or three centuries.

As part of that picture, the awareness of a human right to religious liberty as the basis for a religiously pluralistic society would have to wait; as kind and tolerant as Francis de Sales was personally to the Huguenots he met, theologically and legally he held that heresy or heretical churches as such had no real rights.[1] Only with the Second Vatican Council would official Catholicism recognize the existing situation of other Christian communities and the universal human right and duty to seek the truth in religious matters.[2]

As a result Christians today have possibilities of open dialogue and cooperation that de Sales could only dream about. His zeal for Christian unity, his manifest love for God and all neighbors, and his spirituality itself (which has always had an appeal among Anglicans and Protestants) may yet contribute to greater unity among diverse Christian people.

In describing each of these areas in which Francis de Sales' spirituality needs to be supplemented and updated, I have suggested ways of doing just that—of inserting that spirituality into today's different awarenesses and circumstances. Such insertion promises to be easier for Salesian spirituality than for earlier schools, because it arose on the threshold of the "modern world," and because it was designed largely to be lived in the midst of a changing world.

Furthermore, the very effort of adapting and inserting this spirituality into the world of today is totally in keeping with a key principle of Salesian thinking, with what Francis himself called his "old lesson," so often did he return to it:

> Don't sow your desires in someone else's garden; just culti-
> vate your own as best you can; don't long to be other than what
> you are, but desire to be thoroughly what you are. Direct your

---

1. Cf. Ruth Kleinman, *Saint François de Sales and the Protestants* (Geneva: Droz, 1962). See the basic agreement with her thesis on the part of A. Ravier, *Saint François de Sales, Oeuvres*, pp. lxxiv-lxxviii.

2. See the 1964 *Decree on Ecumenism* and the 1965 *Declaration on Religious Liberty*.

thoughts to being very good at that and to bearing the crosses, little or great, that you will find there. Believe me, this is the most important and least understood point in the spiritual life. We all love what is according to our taste; few people like what is according to their duty or to God's liking. What is the use of building castles in Spain when we have to live in France? This is my old lesson. . . .[1]

To come to accept who you are, where you are, what you are, as a reality intended or at least permitted by a loving God who is present to you right where you are now—that is Francis' old lesson, and it can be extended to accepting when you are. People on the threshold of the twenty-first century cannot live in seventeenth century castles or spiritualities. Only by accepting and living the full reality of the world in which God has placed us can we "give honor to the Master Craftsman whose handiwork we are."[2]

Finally it may be helpful to suggest different models and images to express a spirituality adapted for today. Historically the dominant models and images have been those of Jesus in the solitude of the desert, and of disciples called to leave everything to follow him there or to a life of itinerant preaching. Francis had already pointed out many men and women in the Old and New Testaments and in the post-biblical era who lived holy lives in workshops and families, as soldiers and kings.[3] A contemporary spiritual writer, Thomas Green, has suggested another New Testament figure whose brief story offers a striking contrast to the predominant models with their requirements of leaving all and following Jesus on a journey.[4] It is the story of Zacchaeus, the unlikely one, a wealthy tax-collector, who nevertheless wanted to see Jesus, and found a creative way to do so (Lk 19:1-10). The marvel was that, when Jesus looked up and saw Zacchaeus, he didn't say, "Follow me," but rather: "Zacchaeus, make haste and come down; for I must stay at your house today." Jesus invited himself to dinner and went home with Zacchaeus. There the latter expressed his conversion in terms of four-fold restitution to all he had defrauded, and of giving half of what he owned to the poor.

---

1. Letter to Madame Brûlart, [June] 1607. *Letters of Spiritual Direction*, p. 112.
2. To the same, June 10, 1605: "Let us be what we are and be that well, in order to bring honor to the Master Craftsman whose handiwork we are." *Ibid.*, p. 111.
3. *Introduction* I, 3.
4. Thomas H. Green, S. J., *Come Down Zacchaeus: Spirituality and the Laity* (Notre Dame, Indiana: Ave Maria Press, 1988), especially pp. 9-13.

Jesus' reply was not, "Half is not good enough!" but rather the solemn declaration, "This day salvation has come to this house."

In many ways Salesian spirituality is one of Jesus coming to our homes—to where we live, work, play and pray. It is built on the dwelling of Jesus at home in our hearts through the gift of the Holy Spirit and thus enables us to "find" him wherever we are, in what we do, and in the relationships that form our lives. At the base of it all is the desire to "see" Jesus, and a willingness to risk doing something creative about that desire.

Selections and Translations

In compiling this anthology my purpose has been to make accessible to a wide readership the essential texts of St. Francis de Sales' spirituality, and to do so in a way that respects Francis' own sense of the order and relative importance of topics treated. Pursuit of this goal led to focusing on the heart of the two major works he published, and to respecting the internal order of each. It also led to the discovery in the *Introduction* of an order similar to what is explicit in the *Treatise*, namely, a discussion of prayer or "affective love" and then of life or "effective love." The latter is expressed in the *Introduction* as the virtues needed for holy living, and in the *Treatise* as "living between the one will of God and the other." The reader of the present volume is invited, then, to follow that pattern first at the level of the *Introduction* and again as the pattern recurs in the *Treatise*. Some preliminary pages are taken from the *Introduction* and some concluding chapters from the *Treatise*, while excerpts from Francis' letters have been inserted here and there as they relate to the topics treated in the published works.

In order that this outline be clear throughout, I have inserted headings and subheadings of my own, sometimes subsuming parts of several of Francis' chapters under one heading, at other times suggesting a transition, an emphasis, or an equivalent translation.

Existing translations have been used throughout. That of the *Introduction* is a recent work by three Missionaries of St. Francis de Sales in India. We are grateful to the Indian Institute of Spirituality of Bangalore for allowing this use, and also for permission to make changes deemed helpful to American readers.

The translation of the *Treatise* is that of Vincent Kerns, a British Missionary of St. Francis de Sales, which was published in the United

States by Newman Press in 1962. It is employed here because of its general accuracy and readability and in spite of some expressions which may seem unusual to American readers. Minor changes have been made, mainly for the sake of more inclusive language. We have retained the translator's use of scriptural quotations from the Ronald Knox Bible (Sheed and Ward, 1948), even though the style and some renderings will appear outmoded. The Knox Bible is based on the Latin Vulgate, and follows it in using the Greek Septuagint system of numbering the psalms. We have retained those numbers both when the translator cites a psalm from the Bible and when he adopts the popular "Grail" translation, as a way of paralleling Francis' occasional use of psalms in verse. We have however substituted more recent abbreviations for the books of the Bible, and current spellings of biblical names.

The translation of letters is the work of Sister Peronne Marie Thibert, V.H.M., and comes from the "Classics of Western Spirituality" volume, *Francis de Sales, Jane de Chantal, Letters of Spiritual Direction*, with the kind permission of Paulist Press.

In order that the reader may be able to relate the present selections to any edition or translation of the full text, we refer to Francis' published works by a short title, a Roman numeral indicating the "part" of the *Introduction* or the "book" of the *Treatise*, and an Arabic number indicating the chapter.

For excerpts from the letters, page numbers are those of the Paulist Press volume, abbreviated *Letters*, where references to the French complete works, dates, and other information may be found.

Within any selection, or, in other words, between the references just mentioned, the omission of one or more paragraphs is indicated simply by additional space between the selected paragraphs.

* * *

In October 1893 the first Oblate of St. Francis de Sales to be assigned to the United States arrived in White Plains, New York; may this 1993 publication help in some small way to mark the beginning of the second century of that presence, and to further the diffusion of St. Francis de Sales' spirituality throughout North America.

Joseph F. Power, O.S.F.S.

PART ONE

DEVOUT LIFE

Preliminaries

Those who have written about devotion have nearly all had in mind the instruction of persons completely separated from life in the world. At least, they have taught a kind of devotion leading to such a complete separation. My purpose is to instruct people living in towns, in families, and at court. These are obliged by their state of life to lead an ordinary life to all outward appearances. Very often such persons do not want even to think of venturing on the devout life, finding an excuse in the false claim that it is impossible.

This task is difficult, it is true, and that is why I should like many to give it their attention with greater earnestness than has been shown till now. In spite of my great imperfection, I am trying to provide by means of this book some help to those who will take up this worthy task with a generous heart.

My words are directed to "Philothea." In fact, I want to present for the general benefit of many persons what I had written in the first place for only one. So I use a name which can be given to anyone who wants to lead a devout life. "Philothea" means "one who loves God" or "one who is in love with God."

(*Introduction*, Preface)

Genuine Devotion

You seek devotion, dearest Philothea, because as a Christian you know that it is a virtue very pleasing to God. Small mistakes made at the beginning of any project grow infinitely great as it progresses, and in the end are almost impossible to correct. Hence you should know, before everything else, what is the virtue of devotion.

There is only one true devotion while there is a very large number of false and meaningless ones. So if you cannot recognize true devotion, you could be deceived and waste time in following some devotion that is irrelevant and irrational.

Aurelius used to draw all the faces in the pictures he painted with the expressions and appearance of the women he loved. So each one represents devotion according to his liking and imagination. Those who are in the habit of fasting will think that because they fast they are very devout, even though their hearts are filled with hatred. They will not take a sip of wine, or even of water, anxious about sobriety, but they have no scruples to drink the blood of their neighbors by speaking ill or by false statements.[1] Others consider themselves devout because of the very great number of prayers they recite every day, even though soon after this they speak words that are annoying, full of pride and hurtful to those in their house and to their neighbors. Others very gladly open their purse to give alms to the poor but cannot take any gentleness from their heart to forgive their enemies. Yet others will forgive their enemies but will not pay what they owe unless they are legally forced to do so. All such persons are generally looked upon as devout whereas in fact they are not.

When Saul's soldiers came looking for David in his house, Michal placed a statue on a bed and covered it with David's clothes and so made them believe that it was David himself asleep due to illness (1 Sm 19:11-16). In the same way, many people cover themselves with various external actions related to holy devotion. The world takes them for people who are truly devout and spiritual whereas in reality they are nothing more than statues and illusions of devotion.

Dear Philothea, devotion that is true and living presupposes the love of God, rather it is nothing else than a true love of God. It is not, however, love as such. Insofar as divine love enriches us it is called grace, which makes us pleasing to God. Insofar as it gives us the strength to do good, it is called charity. But when it grows to such a degree of perfection that it makes us not only do good but rather moves us to do it carefully, frequently and promptly, it is called devotion. Ostriches never fly, hens fly only awkwardly, quite low and rarely; but eagles, doves and swallows fly often, swiftly and very high. In the same way, sinners do not fly toward God but rather all their movements are on the earth and for the things of the earth. People who are good, but have not yet come to devotion, fly toward God by their good deeds but rarely, slowly and with difficulty. Persons who are devout fly to God frequently, promptly and freely.

---

1. Literally "by detraction and calumny (slander)."

In short, devotion is nothing else than a spiritual agility and liveliness by means of which charity realizes its actions in us, or we do so by charity, promptly and lovingly.

Just as it is the work of charity to make us keep all the commandments of God in general and without any exception, so it is the work of devotion to make us do so promptly and earnestly. Therefore, whoever does not keep all of God's commandments cannot be considered either good or devout, because to be good one must have charity. To be devout one must not only have charity but a great liveliness and promptness in doing charitable actions.

Since devotion is to be found at a certain level of charity that is extraordinary, it makes us prompt, active and earnest in keeping all of God's commandments. But, more than this, it rouses us to do as many good works as we can, promptly and lovingly, even though they are in no way commanded but rather only counseled or inspired.

Those who have recently recovered from some illness walk as much as they need to, but slowly and with difficulty. So also sinners healed of their sinfulness move ahead to the extent that God commands them, yet slowly and with difficulty until they acquire devotion. After that, like those in good health they not only walk but run joyfully *in the way of God's commandments* (Ps 118:32). Even more, they move ahead and run in the paths of God's counsels and inspirations.

In conclusion, charity and devotion are not more different from each other than the flame from the fire, all the more so because charity is a spiritual fire which when it burns with intense flames is called devotion. In fact, devotion adds to the fire of charity only the flame which makes charity prompt, active and diligent not only to keep God's commandments but also to put into practice his counsels and inspirations.

(*Introduction* I, 1)

Varieties of Devotion for Varieties of People

God commanded the plants, at the creation, to bear fruit *each according to its kind* (Gn 1:11). Similarly, he commands Christians, the living plants of his Church, to produce the fruits of devotion according to each one's ability and occupation.

Devotion is to be practiced differently by the nobleman, the worker, the servant, the prince, the widow, the young girl, the wife. Even more than this, the practice of devotion has to be adapted to the strength, life-situation and duties of each individual.

Do you think, dear Philothea, that it is suitable for a bishop to desire to live the life of a hermit like a Carthusian monk? If people with a family were to want to be like the Capuchins not acquiring any property, if a worker spent a great deal of time in church like the member of a religious order, and if a religious was always subject to being disturbed in all sorts of ways for the service of his neighbor like a bishop, would not such devotion be ridiculous, disorderly and intolerable? However, this sort of fault is very common. The world, which does not distinguish or does not want to distinguish between devotion and the indiscretion of those who consider themselves devout, complains and finds fault with devotion which is in no way responsible for such disorders.

Indeed, Philothea, devotion in no way spoils anything if it be true; rather it makes everything perfect. When it conflicts with any person's legitimate occupation, it is without doubt false. "The bee," says Aristotle, "sucks honey from flowers without damaging them," leaving them as whole and fresh as it found them. But true devotion does even better. Not only does it not spoil any sort of life-situation or occupation, but on the contrary enriches it and makes it attractive. All sorts of precious stones when immersed in honey have a greater brilliance, each according to its color. Similarly, everyone becomes more pleasant in one's state of life by joining it with devotion. Devotion makes the care of the family peaceful, the love of husband and wife more sincere, the service of the ruler more loyal, and every sort of occupation more pleasant and more loveable.

It is an error, or rather, a heresy, to try to exclude the devout life from the soldiers' regiment, the workers' shop, the court of rulers or the home of the married. It is true, Philothea, that a devotion which is purely contemplative, monastic and religious cannot be practiced in such occupations. However, besides these three sorts of devotion, there are many others suitable for leading to perfection those who live their lives in the world.

(Introduction I, 3)

Letters about Devotion

To Madame Brulart

I advise you to take the trouble now and then to visit hospitals, to comfort the sick, and to have compassion for their infirmities, letting these touch your heart; and pray for the sick even as you give them whatever help you can. But in all this, be very careful that your husband, your servants, and your relatives be not inconvenienced by overly long visits to church, by too lengthy withdrawals to pray and noticeable neglect of your household responsibilities or, as sometimes happens, by your trying to control the actions of others, or showing too much disdain for gatherings where the rules of devotion are not precisely observed. In all these instances charity must prevail and enlighten us so that we yield to the wishes of our neighbor in whatever is not contrary to the commandments of God.

You must not only be devout and love devotion, but you must render it lovable to everyone. Now you will make it lovable if you render it useful and pleasing. The sick will love your devotion if they receive care and comfort from it; your family will love it if they see you more attentive to their well-being, more gentle in handling affairs, more kind in correcting, and so on; your husband will love it if he sees that as your devotion increases, you become more warm and affectionate toward him; your relatives and friends will love it if they see you more free, supportive of others, and yielding to them in matters that are not contrary to God's will. In short, we must, as far as possible, make our devotion attractive.

(Letters, p. 104)

As for your desire to see your dear ones make progress in the service of God and in their longing for Christian perfection, I praise this desire of yours tremendously and, since you wish it, shall add my poor prayers to your supplications to God for this intention. But to tell you the truth, I am always afraid that in these desires which are not of the essence of our salvation and perfection, there may be a trace of self-love and self-will; for example, we may indulge so much in these desires which are not really essential that we may not leave enough room in our hearts for those that are: humility, resignation, gentleness of heart, and the like. Or else the intensity of these desires may bring about anxiety and overeagerness, and in the end we do not submit ourselves to God's will as perfectly as we should.

This is what I fear in such desires. That's why I beg you to be very careful to avoid these dangers and to pursue your aim gently and quietly, that is to say, without upsetting those with whom you would like to share your desire for perfection. Do not even tell them what you hope for, because, believe me, this would do more harm than good. By what you say and do you must gently sow seeds which might sway them to your views; without pretending to want to teach them or win them over, gradually plant holy inspirations and reflections in their minds. In this way, especially if you pray about it too, you will do more good than you would in any other way.

(*Letters*, p. 110)

To Madame de Limojon

And how happy you will be if in the midst of the world you keep Jesus Christ in your heart! I beg him to live and rule there eternally.

Keep in mind the main lesson he left us—in *three* words so that we would never forget it and could repeat it a hundred times a day: *Learn of me,* he said, *that I am gentle and humble of heart.* That says it all: to have a heart gentle toward one's neighbor and humble toward God. At every moment give this heart, the very heart of your heart, to our Savior. You will see that as this divine, delicate lover takes his place in your heart, the world with its vanities and superfluities will leave.

I have said this to you in person, madam, and now I write it: I don't want a devotion that is bizarre, confused, neurotic, strained, and sad, but rather, a gentle, attractive, peaceful piety; in a word, a piety that is quite spontaneous and wins the love of God, first of all, and after that, the love of others.

(*Letters*, p. 156)

Praying

The Importance of Prayer

Prayer is opening our understanding to God's brightness and light, and exposing our will to the warmth of his love. Nothing else purifies so well our understanding of its ignorance and our will of its sinful attachments. It is a spring of blessings and its waters quench the thirst of the passions of our heart, wash away our imperfections, and make the plants of our good desires grow green and bear flowers.

I strongly recommend to you prayer of the mind and of the heart, and especially that based on the life and passion of our Lord. By looking upon him often in meditation, your whole being will be filled with him. You will learn his attitudes and model your actions on his.

He is *the light of the world* (Jn 8:12), and therefore we must be enlightened and instructed in him, by him and for him. He is the tree of desire in whose shade we must seek refreshment (Sg 2:3). He is the living *well of Jacob* (Jn 4:6) for the cleansing of all our stains.

Children learn to speak by constantly listening to their mothers and chattering to them. So we, remaining close to the Savior in meditation and observing his words, his actions, and his loving desires, shall learn with the help of his grace to speak, act and will like him.

(Introduction II, 1)

A Simple Method of Meditating

Preparation

Perhaps, Philothea, you do not know how to practice mental prayer. Unfortunately, it is something that few people know nowadays. So I will teach you a short and simple method for it. It will be of help until you are more fully instructed by reading the numerous good books on this subject, and above all by practice.

I begin with the preparation which consists of two points: the first is to place oneself in the presence of God, and the second is to ask for his help. I suggest four principal ways of placing yourself in the presence of God which you can use for this preparation.

The first consists in a lively and attentive awareness of the omnipresence of God: God is in everything and everywhere; there is no place or thing in this world where he is not very really present. Just as the birds always find the air wherever they fly, so wherever we go or wherever we are, we find God present. This truth is known to everyone, but not everyone is attentive to it to be conscious of it.

The second way of placing yourself in the presence of God is to reflect that God is present not only in the place where you are, but that he is very specially present in your heart and in the very center of your spirit. He enlivens and animates it by his divine presence, being there as the heart of your heart and the spirit of your spirit. The soul is spread throughout the entire body, and is present in every part of it, yet resides in a particular manner in the heart. Similarly, God who is indeed present everywhere, is present in a special way in our spirit. Hence David calls God *the God of his heart* (Ps 73:26), and St. Paul says that *we live and move and are in God* (Acts 17:28). Considering this truth you will awaken in your heart a deep reverence for God who is so intimately present there.

The third way is to think of our Savior, who in his humanity sees from heaven all the persons in the world, but particularly Christians who are his children and most specially those who are at prayer, whose actions and behavior he notices. This is not mere imagination but a most certain truth. Though we do not see him, yet he looks at us from on high. St. Stephen, at the time of his martyrdom, saw him in this way (Acts 7:55). So we can truly say with the Spouse: *Look, there he is behind the wall, gazing in at the windows, looking through the lattice* (Sg 2:9).

The fourth way consists in using simple imagination to represent our Savior in his sacred humanity, as if he were near us, just as we are used to imagining our friends and saying, "I imagine I can see a certain person doing this or that, it seems to me that I see him," or some such things.

But if the most holy sacrament of the altar is present, then this presence will be real and not merely imaginary. The species and appearance of bread is like a tapestry, from behind which our Lord really present sees and observes us, though we cannot see him as he is.

Make use of one of these four ways to place yourself in the presence of God before prayer. Do not try to use them all together. Use only one at a time and that briefly and simply.

(Introduction II, 2)

The invocation is made as follows: Having become aware that you are in the presence of God, cast yourself down with profound reverence. Acknowledge that you are most unworthy to remain before such a supreme Lord. Yet, knowing that his Goodness desires it, ask him for the grace to serve and adore him well in this meditation.

You may use, if you wish, some short and fervent words, like these of David: *Do not cast me away, my God, from your face, and do not take from me the favor of your Holy Spirit* (Ps 51:11). *Let your face shine on your servant* (Ps 31:16), *and I will see your wonders* (Ps 119:18). *Give me understanding and I will consider your law, and keep it with my whole heart* (Ps 119:34). *I am your servant, give me understanding* (Ps 119:125), and similar words.

(Introduction II, 3)

Besides these two general points to prepare for meditation, there is a third which is not common to every sort of mediation. Some call it the composition of place, and others the interior presentation. This consists in presenting to one's imagination the scene of the mystery taken for meditation, as if it was really and truly taking place before us. For example, if you wish to meditate on our Lord on the cross, imagine that you are on Mount Calvary seeing and hearing all that was done and said on the day of the passion. Or, if you wish, for it is the same thing, imagine that in the very place where you are the crucifixion of our Lord is being done, in the way the evangelists describe it.

(Introduction II, 4)

Reflections

Having made use of the imagination, next make use of the understanding. This is what we call meditation. It consists in making one or many reflections in order to arouse good movements of the will toward God and the things of God. In this, meditation differs from study or other thoughts and reflections which are made, not to acquire virtue or the love of God, but for some other purposes and intentions, such as to become learned, to write or to take part in a discussion.

Hence, after confining your spirit, as I have said, within the limits of the subject on which you wish to meditate, either by using the imagination if it is something perceptible to the senses, or by a simple presentation if it is not, begin to reflect on it. . . .

As long as you find sufficient attraction, light and fruit in one of these reflections, stop there without moving on to another. Be like the bees who do not leave a flower as long as they find honey to gather there. But if a reflection is not to your liking, after attending to it and trying it for a while, pass on to another. But go on very gently and simply in this matter, without any hurry.

(Introduction II, 5)

Good Movements of the Will and Deliberate Decisions[1]

Meditation produces good movements in the will, such as the love of God and of our neighbor; the desire of heaven and eternal glory; zeal for the salvation of others; imitation of the life of our Lord; compassion, admiration, joy; fear of God's displeasure, of judgment, and of hell; hatred of sin; confidence in the goodness and mercy of God, shame for the sins of our past life. Our spirit should give vent whole-heartedly to these good movements of the will.

But Philothea, do not linger too long with these general good movements of the will. You have to change them into deliberate decisions, precise and particular, for your correction and improvement.

For example, the first words spoken by our Lord on the cross will surely arouse in you a good movement of the will to imitate him. That is, you will desire to forgive your enemies and to love them. But I want to make it clear that this will be of little value unless you make a particular deliberate decision like the following: "I will not take offence anymore at such or such annoying words which such or such a person—my neighbor or my servant—may say about me"; or "I will not be displeased

---

1. The title is literally "Affections and Resolutions," technical religious terms whose precise sense has become obscured. The phrase, "good movements of the will" is taken literally from the first line in this chapter and will be substituted throughout for "affections," while "deliberate decisions" is used for "resolutions."

any more by this or that insult from this or that person"; and "on the contrary, I will say and do such or such a thing in order to win the person over and make him friendly"; and so on with regard to other matters.

In this way, Philothea, you will correct your faults in a short time. But with only the good movements of the will, you will do so after a long time and with difficulty.

(Introduction II, 6)

Conclusion

Bring the meditation to a close with three acts which must be made with as much humility as possible:

1. The first is an *act of thanksgiving.* We thank God for the good movements of the will and the deliberate decisions he has given us and for his goodness and mercy which we have discovered in the mystery on which we have been meditating.

2. The second is an *act of oblation.* We offer to God his goodness and mercy, and the death, the suffering, and the virtues of his Son, and along with these, our own good movements of the will and our deliberate decisions.

3. The third is an *act of petition.* We ask God and implore him to give us the graces and virtues of his Son, and to bless our good movements of the will and our deliberate decisions so that we can practice them faithfully. We pray also for the church, for our pastors, for our relatives and friends and others. We ask our Lady, the angels and the saints to intercede for us. Lastly, as I have already mentioned, we should pray the Our Father and the Hail Mary, the general and necessary prayers for all the faithful.

I have also suggested that, after all this, we should gather a little nosegay of devotion. I shall now explain what I mean. After taking a walk in a beautiful garden, people hesitate to leave without taking four or five flowers in order to enjoy their fragrance the rest of the day. Similarly, having considered some mystery in meditation, we should pick one or two or three ideas in which we took special delight and which are more helpful to our improvement. We should remind ourselves of them during the day, breathing in their spiritual fragrance. This nosegay of spiritual thoughts is to be gathered while we are still in the place where we made our meditation, or as we walk about alone for some time soon after.

(Introduction II, 7)

Advice about Meditation

It is of the greatest importance, Philothea, that after your meditation you keep in mind the deliberate decisions and plans you have made in order to put them into practice carefully during that very day. This is the principal fruit of meditation. Without it, meditation is very often not only useless but even harmful. In fact, merely to meditate on virtues and not to practice them, sometimes makes our minds and our emotions swell with pride. We are convinced that we are in fact what we have resolved and decided to be. This may be true without doubt if your deliberate decisions are earnest and determined. However, they are not such but rather useless and dangerous if they are not put into practice.

Therefore, we must try in every way we can to practice our deliberate decisions, looking out for opportunities, small or great. For example, I am firmly determined to change, by my gentleness, the attitude of those who insult me. I shall try to meet them that very day, in order to greet them in a friendly way. In case I do not come across them, I will at least speak well of them and pray to God for them.

On finishing this earnest prayer, take care not to give your heart a sudden jerk which will spill the balm you have received by means of the prayer. I mean, you must keep silence for some time if you can, and move your heart very gently from prayer to your occupations. Keep the feelings and good movements of the will produced in you for as long as possible.

A man is given some liquid of great value to take home in a bowl of beautiful porcelain. He will walk carefully, not looking to one side or the other. He will look sometimes in front, for fear of tripping over a stone or making a false step. Sometimes, he will look at his bowl to see that it is not leaning to one side. After finishing your meditation, you must behave in the same way. Do not become distracted all of a sudden, but look simply ahead. For instance, if you must meet someone to whom you have to speak or listen, this is unavoidable. Adjust yourself to it, but in such a way that you also take care of your heart. Thus as little as possible of the precious liquid of holy prayer will be lost.

Even more, you must get used to being able to pass from prayer to all kinds of activities which your occupation and way of life require of you, honestly and rightly, though they seem far removed from the good movements of the will received in prayer. I mean, the lawyer must be able to pass from prayer to his work in court, the shopkeeper to his business, the married woman to her duties in her family and the bother of her household tasks, with so much gentleness and peacefulness that their minds are not disturbed in any way. Prayer as well as other duties are according to the will of God. So passing from one to the other must be done in a spirit of humility and devotion.

Sometimes it may happen that, immediately after the preparation for meditation, your good movements of the will are wholly aroused toward God. At such times, Philothea, give vent to them freely and do not try to follow the method I have presented to you. Usually, reflection must precede good movements of the will and deliberate decisions. But if the Holy Spirit produces in you good movements of the will before the reflection, you must not look for the reflection since it is made only to arouse the good movements of the will. In short, whenever the good movements of the will present themselves to you, you must welcome them and make room for them, whether they come before or after all the reflections.

Although I have placed the good movements of the will after all the reflections, I have done so only the better to mark the different parts of prayer. Nevertheless, it is a general rule that we must never hold back the good movements of the will. Rather we must give expression to them freely when they present themselves. I say this not only regarding the other good movements of the will but also as regards the act of thanksgiving, the act of oblation and the act of petition, which can be made among the reflections. These must not be controlled any more than the other good movements of the will. But later, when concluding the meditation, it is necessary to take them up again and repeat them.

(*Introduction* II, 8)

Recalling God's Presence during the Day

Regarding this exercise, dear Philothea, I want you to follow my advice with great earnestness. In fact, in this practice is contained one of the most sure means of your spiritual progress.

In the course of the day, recall to mind the presence of God, as often as you can. Use one of the four ways I have shown you. Become aware of what God is doing and of what you are doing: you will realize that his eyes are turned toward you and, with unparalleled love, fixed on you all the time. "My God," you will say, "why do I not look at you always, as you look at me always? You think of me so often, my Lord, and I think of you so seldom. Where am I? My true place is God, and where do I find myself?"

So keep in mind, Philothea, always to recollect yourself again and again in the solitude of your heart, while outwardly dealing with others and your occupations. This spiritual solitude cannot be prevented by the many people who are around you. They are not around your heart but only around your body. So your heart can remain by itself all alone, in the presence of God alone.

So recollect your spirit within your heart every now and then. There, separated from everyone, you can speak to God heart to heart about yourself.

(Introduction II, 12)

This exercise is not difficult. It can be interwoven with all our occupations and work without causing the least disturbance. All the more so because, both in the awareness of God's presence and in these interior longings, we turn aside only in a small way and briefly. This is no obstacle, but rather helps us very much to continue what we are doing. The pilgrim takes a little wine to give joy to his heart and to refresh his mouth. Even though he stops for some time to do this, he does not end his journey. Rather, he finds strength to complete it with greater speed and ease. He stops in order to go on better.

Many have made a collection of numerous vocal ejaculatory prayers which are no doubt very helpful. However, I advise you not to force yourself to use any particular words. Rather, say in your heart or aloud those which love prompts at the time, for it will inspire you with as many as you want. It is true that certain words have a special ability to delight the heart in this respect. Such are the ejaculatory prayers scattered in such abundance throughout the Psalms of David, as also the various invocations of the name of Jesus and the darts of love to be found in the Song of Songs. Hymns are also helpful for this purpose, provided they are sung with attention.

In brief, men in love with a human and natural love have their thoughts turned, almost always, toward the person they love. Their heart is full of affection for her. They always speak her praises. In her absence, they lose no opportunity to express their love through letters. They carve her name on the bark of every tree they find. Similarly, those who love God cannot stop thinking of him, seeking him, longing for him and speaking of him. They would engrave, if it were possible, the holy and sacred name of Jesus on the breast of every person in the world.

To the above, they are invited by every creature. There is not a single creature which does not proclaim the praise of their dearly Beloved. As St. Augustine says, following St. Anthony, everything in the world speaks to them, in a language that is silent but full of meaning, about the one they love. All things stir up good thoughts in them and these are the source, later on, of numerous longings for God and ejaculatory prayers.

In this exercise of the awareness of God's presence and of ejaculatory prayers is to be found the most important practice of devotion. It can make up for the lack of all other prayers. But to make good its absence, by any other means, is almost impossible. Without this exercise, the contemplative life cannot be well lived, and the active life will be lived only badly. Without it, relaxation is only idleness and work only discomfort. Therefore, I ask you earnestly, take up this exercise with all your heart and never stop practicing it.

(Introduction II, 13)

Letters about Prayer

To Mademoiselle de Soulfour

The uneasiness that you experience at prayer, together with your anxiety to find a subject that can captivate and satisfy your mind, is in itself enough to prevent you from finding what you seek. When we are too intent in our search for something, we can look at it a hundred times without seeing it.

Such useless anxiety can only result in weariness of mind which in turn produces this coldness and numbness in your soul. I don't know what remedies you should apply, but I do think you would gain a great deal if you could keep from being so anxious, for that is one of the greatest obstacles to devotion and real virtue. It pretends to incite us to good, but all it does is cool our ardor; it makes us run, only to have us stumble. That's why we have to be on guard against it at all times, especially during prayer.

And to help you be vigilant in this, remind yourself that the graces and benefits of prayer are not like water welling up from the earth, but more like water coming down from heaven; therefore all our efforts cannot produce them, though it is true that we must ready ourselves to receive them with great care, yet humbly and peacefully. We must keep our hearts open and wait for the heavenly dew to fall. Never forget to carry this thought with you to prayer: in prayer we approach God and place ourselves in his presence for two reasons.

The first is to render to God the honor and praise we owe him, and this can be done without his speaking to us or our speaking to him. We can fulfill this duty by acknowledging that he is our God and we, his lowly creatures, and by remaining before him, prostrate in spirit, awaiting his orders. How many courtiers there are who go into the presence of the king over and over again, not to speak to him or listen to him speak, but just to be seen by him and to indicate by their regular appearance that they are his servants! This aim we have in presenting ourselves before God simply to demonstrate and prove our willingness and gratitude to be in his service is excellent, very holy and very pure, and, therefore, a mark of great perfection.

The second reason why we present ourselves before God is to speak to him and to hear him speak to us through inspirations and the inner stirrings of our heart. Ordinarily, we take great delight in doing this because it is very beneficial for us to speak to such a great Lord; and when he answers us, he pours out much balm and precious ointment, and in this way fills our soul with tremendous consolation.

So, Mademoiselle, my dear daughter (since this is how you want me to address you), one or other of these two benefits can never be absent from your prayer. If we are able to speak to our Lord, let us do so; let us praise him, pray to him, listen to him. If we are unable to speak because our voice fails us, let us, nevertheless, stay in the hall of the king and bow down before him; he will see us there, will graciously accept our patience, and look with favor on our silence. Another time we will be very surprised when he takes us by the hand, chats with us, and walks with us up and down in his garden of prayer; and even if he never does this, let us be satisfied that it is our duty to be in his entourage and that it is a great grace and a still greater honor that he allows us to be in his presence. In this way, we won't be overeager to speak to him because this other manner of being near him is no less useful to us and, in fact, may be more so, although not so much to our taste.

So when you come before the Lord, talk to him if you can; if you can't just stay there, let yourself be seen, and don't try too hard to do anything else.

(Letters, pp. 100-01)

To Madame Brulart

You tell me you do nothing at all in prayer. But what would you want to do that you are not already doing, that is, presenting and re-presenting your nothingness and your misery to God. The most eloquent appeal that beggars make is to show us their sores and their neediness. But sometimes, you tell me, you can't even do that much and just stay there like a shadow or a statue. Well, that in itself is no small achievement. In the palaces of princes and kings there are statues that serve only to please the eye of the prince; be satisfied then to serve the same purpose in the presence of God. He will bring the statue to life when he chooses.

Trees bear fruit only because of the presence of the sun, some sooner, some later, some every year, and others every three years, not all of them always yielding equal harvests. We are very fortunate to be able to remain in the presence of God; so let us be content that he will make us bear our fruit sooner or later, every day or only occasionally, according to his good pleasure to which we should be fully resigned.

(Letters, pp. 108-09)

Living

Virtues and Non-virtues

Music, so pleasant in itself, *is out of place in time of mourning,* says the Proverb (Sir 22:6). It is a great fault in many who undertake the practice of a particular virtue to insist on turning out acts of it on any and every occasion. Like some of the ancient philosophers they wish either to weep always or to laugh always. Still worse, they criticize and condemn those who do not practice these same virtues at all times as they do. The apostle says: *Rejoice with those who rejoice, weep with those who weep* (Rom 12:15); *charity is patient, kind* (1 Cor 13:4), generous, prudent and lowers itself willingly.

Nevertheless there are virtues which are almost always practiced. These must not only produce their own acts but must also communicate their quality to the acts of all other virtues. Occasions of practicing courage, magnanimity and great generosity are rare. But gentleness, moderation, honesty and humility are some of the virtues by which every action of our life should be colored. The practice of these are more necessary, though there are virtues which are more excellent. Sugar is more enjoyable than salt but salt has a more frequent and more general use. We must always have a good store of these general virtues at hand since we ought to make constant use of them.

(*Introduction* III, 1)

There are certain things which many consider as virtues but are not such at all. I must say a word about them: these are ecstasies or raptures, experiences of insensibility, impassability, deific unions, levitations, transformations and other such perfections treated in some books. They promise to raise the soul to purely intellectual contemplation, to a total concentration of the spirit and to a supereminent life. You see, Philothea, such perfections are not virtues. Rather they are rewards which God gives for virtues. Better still, they are a foretaste of the happiness of the life to come given sometimes to people to make them long for its fullness in

46

paradise. But for all that we must not seek such graces since they are in no way necessary for serving and loving God well, which ought to be our sole aim.

Often these are not graces which can be acquired by one's own effort and skill since they are more passive than active. We can receive them but not create them in us. I add that we have only undertaken to make ourselves good persons, persons committed to devotion, devout men and women. Therefore we must work hard for it. If it pleases God to elevate us to such angelic perfection, we shall be also good angels.

While awaiting, let us simply, humbly and devoutly exercise ourselves in small virtues the conquest of which our Lord has entrusted to our care and toil: such as patience, good-naturedness, mortifications of the heart, humility, obedience, poverty, chastity, tenderness toward our neighbor, bearing their imperfections, diligence and holy fervor.

Certainly, very high and lofty desires for extraordinary graces are greatly subject to illusions, deceptions and errors. Sometimes it happens that those who esteem themselves to be angels are not even good people and in fact there is more of greatness in the words and terms they use than in their sentiments and deeds. All the same, we must not rashly condemn or blame anything. While blessing God for the supereminence of others, let us be firm on our way: lower but safer, less excellent but more suited to our insufficiency and littleness. If we continue in it, humbly and faithfully, God will raise us to great heights which are great indeed.

(*Introduction* III, 2)

The "Little" Virtues Needed Everywhere

Patience

You have need of patience so that doing the will of God you may receive what he has promised (Heb 10:36), says the apostle. Yes, for as the Savior had declared, *You shall possess yourself in patience* (Lk 21:19). It is the great happiness of human beings, Philothea, to be in possession of ourselves. The more perfect our patience, the more perfectly we possess ourselves. Often recall to your mind that our Lord saved us by his sufferings and endurance. In the same way, we must work out our salvation by sufferings, trials, bearing insults, conflicts and troubles with as much gentleness as possible.

Do not limit your patience to this or that kind of insults and trials but extend it without exception to all that God will send you or allow to happen to you. Some wish to suffer only trials which are honorable, for example: to be wounded in battle, to be prisoners of war, to be ill-treated for the sake of religion, to be impoverished by some lawsuit in which they are successful. Such persons do not love the trials but the honor they bring. The really patient servant of God bears with equanimity the humiliating trials as well as the honorable.

To be despised, criticized and accused by the wicked, this is entirely pleasant to a person of courage. But to be criticized, accused and ill-treated by good people, by friends, by relations is a real test of virtue. I admire more the gentleness with which the great St. Charles Borromeo suffered for a long time the public criticisms addressed to him in the pulpit by a great preacher of a strictly reformed order than all the attacks which he endured from others. Just as the stings of bees are more painful than those of flies, so too the harm we receive from good people and their opposition are more unbearable than others. Yet such situations often arise: two good persons both with good intentions stir up great trials and conflicts against one another due to the differences of their opinions.

Be patient not only in the main and important details of the misfortunes which may come upon you but also as regards the secondary and accidental circumstances which flow from them. Many would be willing to accept trouble provided they were not in any way inconvenienced. "I would not be troubled at being poor," says one, "if it did not prevent me from serving my friends, educating my children and living honorably as I would like to." Another says: "I would not care about being poor if the people did not think that it happened to me due to my fault." Another would be quite glad to be calumniated and would bear it patiently provided no one believed the slanderer. Others would be willing, it seems, to put up with some of the inconvenience of illness, but not all of it. They are not impatient at being ill, they say, but at not having the money for treatment, or at being a bother to those around them. Now I say, Philothea, we must have patience not only at being ill, but also at being ill with the illness which God wishes, in the place where he wishes and among the persons he wishes, and also with the discomforts he wishes. The same is to be said about other trials.

When any evil happens to you, make use of such means which are possible in accordance with God's will. To do otherwise would be to tempt the divine majesty. After taking the means, await the outcome which is pleasing to God with complete resignation. If it pleases him that the means overcome the evil, then thank him with humility. But if it pleases him that the evil overcomes the means, then bless him with patience.

I am of the same opinion as St. Gregory: when you are rightly accused of some fault that you have committed, humble yourself very much and acknowledge that you deserve the accusation brought against you. If you are falsely accused, excuse yourself gently denying your guilt because you owe this respect to the truth and to the edification of your neighbor. But even if, after your genuine and legitimate excuse, they continue to accuse you, do not be at all troubled and do nothing to get your excuse accepted. For after doing your duty to the truth, you ought to do it also to humility. In this way, you neither offend against the care you owe to your good name, or the affection you owe to tranquility, gentleness of heart and humility.

Complain as little as possible about the wrongs done to you. For it is certain that in general the one who complains, sins insofar as self-love makes us feel the offenses to be greater than they really are. Above all do not make your complaints to persons inclined to be indignant or to think rashly. If it is expedient for you to complain to someone either to correct an offence or to restore your peace of mind, then let it be to peaceful persons who really love God. Otherwise instead of calming your heart, they will stir it up to greater anxieties; instead of taking away the thorn which pricks you, they will drive it deeper into your foot.

Truly patient people neither complain about suffering nor seek pity. They speak of it unaffectedly, truthfully and simply, without lamenting, without complaining and without exaggerating. If we pity them, they patiently allow themselves to be pitied, except when they are pitied for an affliction they do not have. While they simply declare that they have no such suffering, they remain in a peaceful state between truth and patience, admitting the evil but not complaining about it.

When you meet with difficulties in the exercise of devotion, and these will not be wanting, remember the words of our Lord: *A woman has great anguish when she is in labor, but seeing the child that is born she forgets her suffering for joy that a human being is born into the world* (Jn 16:21).

In fact, you have within yourself the most noble child in the world who is Jesus Christ. Until he is formed and brought forth, you cannot but feel great pain. But be of good courage. These sorrows will pass away and eternal joy will remain for bringing forth such a child into the world. Then he will be brought forth entirely for you, when you have formed him completely in your heart and in your works by imitating his life.

When you fall sick offer all your sorrows, pains and weaknesses to the service of our Lord and implore him to join them to the torments he suffered for you. Obey your doctor, take the medicines, food and other remedies for the love of God, remembering the gall he took for love of you. Desire to be healed for the sake of serving him. Do not refuse to be sick in order to obey him and prepare yourself for death if such is his will that you may praise him and rejoice with him.

Remember that the bees at the time of making honey live and feed on very bitter food. Similarly we cannot make acts of the greatest gentleness and patience nor compose the honey of excellent virtues except by eating the bread of bitterness and living amidst trials. As honey made out of the flowers of thyme, a small bitter herb, is the best of all, so also the virtues practiced in the bitterness of the most vile, low and mean trials and humiliations are the most excellent of all.

Look often with your interior eyes on Jesus Christ crucified, naked, blasphemed, slandered, abandoned and overwhelmed by every kind of trouble, sorrow and pain. Consider that all your sufferings are not comparable to his either in quality or in quantity; you will never be able to suffer anything for his sake compared to what he suffered for you. Consider the torments endured by the martyrs of old and those so many people suffer now are incomparably more severe than yours and say: Alas! my sufferings are comforts and my thorns are roses in comparison with those who without help, without assistance and without relief live in continual death weighed down by afflictions infinitely greater than mine.

(*Introduction* III, 3)

Humility

Vainglory is the glory we give ourselves for what is not in us, or for what is in us but is not ours, or what is in us and is ours but for which we do not deserve any credit. Nobility of race, the favor of the great and popularity are not in us but either in our predecessors or in the esteem of others. Some feel themselves proud and haughty because they ride on a good horse, have a feather in their cap or are splendidly attired. But who does not see that all this is folly? If there is any glory in these things, it belongs to the horse, to the bird and to the tailor. What meanness to borrow one's esteem from a horse, from a feather or from a garment.

Some take pride in their turned-up moustaches, well-trimmed beards, curled hair, soft hands, in their ability to dance, play or sing. Are they not showing lack of courage in seeking to enhance their value and increase their reputation through such trifling and silly things? Some wish to be honored and respected by people for a little learning as if everyone ought to become their pupils and hold them as masters; they are, therefore, called pedants. Some strut like peacocks thinking they are beautiful and believe everyone is courting them. All this is extremely vain, foolish, insolent, and the glory based on such silly things is called vain, foolish, frivolous.

We know genuine goodness like we know genuine balm. We test the balm by pouring it in water. If it goes to the bottom and takes the lowest place it is judged to be the finest and most precious. Similarly to know whether someone is truly wise, learned, generous, noble, we ought to see whether these good qualities tend to humility, modesty and submission for then they will be really good. If they float on the surface and wish to show themselves then, the more showy they are, the less genuine will they be. Pearls conceived and nourished in wind and the noise of thunder are only shells devoid of substance. In the same way, the virtues and the good qualities which are received and nourished in arrogance, boastfulness and vanity have only the appearance of good without sap, without marrow and without firmness.

Honors, ranks and dignities are like saffron which grows better and flourishes when trampled underfoot. It is not an honor to be handsome when one is concerned about it. Beauty to be graceful must be unaffected. Knowledge dishonors us when it puffs us up and degenerates into pedantry. If we are bickering for ranks, precedence and titles, besides exposing our qualities to examination, investigation and conflict, we make them mean and contemptible. Honor received as a gift is excellent but becomes mean when exacted, sought after and demanded.

(*Introduction* III, 4)

You desire, Philothea, that I lead you further in humility. For to do as I have already proposed is rather wisdom than humility; now I pass on further. Many neither wish nor dare to think and reflect upon the graces God has given them personally, for fear of vainglory and self-complacency. In this, they certainly deceive themselves. As the great Angelic Doctor[1] says, the true means of attaining to the love of God is the consideration of his blessings. The more we know them the more we shall love him. Since the gifts received personally move us more powerfully than those shared in common, they are also to be considered more attentively.

Nothing indeed can humble us so much before the mercy of God as the multitude of his benefits, and nothing can humble us so deeply before his justice as the multitude of our misdeeds. Let us consider what he has done for us and what we have done against him. As we consider in detail our sins so also let us reflect in detail on the graces he has given us. There is no need to fear that the knowledge of the gifts bestowed on us will make us proud provided we are attentive to the truth that the good that is in us is not from us. Alas! the mules do not cease to be clumsy and disgusting beasts even when laden with the precious and perfumed goods of the prince. What good do we have that we have not received? If we have received then why are we proud (1 Cor 4:7)? On the contrary, a lively consideration of the graces received makes us humble, for recognition of them begets gratitude.

But if the knowledge of the graces God gave us arouses some kind of vanity in us, the sure remedy is to have recourse to the consideration of our ingratitude, our imperfections and our miseries. If we reflect on what we have done when God was not with us, then we shall realize well that what we do when he is with us is not our work or of our thinking. We shall be happy and we shall rejoice in our deeds because we have done them, but we shall glorify God alone because he is their author. Thus the Holy Virgin proclaims that God has done great things for her but it is only to humble herself and glorify God: *my soul*, she says, *exalts the Lord because he has done great things for me* (Lk 1:46, 49).

We often say that we are nothing, that we are misery itself and the refuse of the world. But we would be very sorry if anyone took us at our word and made public that we are such. On the contrary, we make a show of running away and hiding ourselves so that we are pursued and sought

---

1. Honorific title given to St. Thomas Aquinas (1225-74) since the fifteenth century.

after. We pretend to wish to be the last, and seated at the lower end of the table, but it is only to pass to the top with greater advantage. Genuine humility does not make a show of itself. It scarcely says words of humility because it does not only wish to hide the other virtues but also and especially seeks to hide itself. If it were lawful to lie, to pretend, or to scandalize one's neighbor, humility would produce arrogant and proud actions in order to hide itself under them and to live there altogether unknown and concealed.

My advice, then, Philothea is that either let us not use expressions of humility at all, or say them with true interior awareness in keeping with what we utter externally. Let us never lower our eyes without humbling our hearts. Let us not make a show of wanting to be the last unless we really wish it.

(*Introduction* III, 5)

Praise, honor and glory are not given to people for ordinary virtue but for outstanding virtue. For by praise we wish to persuade others to appreciate someone's excellence. By honor we declare that we ourselves esteem that person. Glory, in my opinion, is the aura which results from the accumulation of many praises and honors; the latter are like precious stones which, when accumulated, result in glory like a sparkling enamel.

Now humility does not allow us to have any desire of excelling others or of having the right to be preferred to others. It will not permit us to seek after praise, honor and glory which are due only to excellence. But it agrees with the warning of the Wise Man who admonishes us *to have care for our good name* (Sir 41:15) because a good name is an esteem not of excellence but only of a simple honesty and integrity of life. Humility does not prevent us from recognizing these qualities in ourselves and as a consequence desiring a reputation for them. It is true that humility would despise a good name if charity had no need of it. However, a good name is one of the foundations of human society and without it we are not only useless but harmful to the public because of the scandal it would cause. Charity requires and humility agrees that we must desire to have it and preserve it carefully.

The leaves of trees are of no great value in themselves. All the same they are of great use not only to beautify the trees but also to protect the fruits when they are still tender. So too, a good name, not very desirable in itself, remains very useful. It not only adorns our life but also preserves our virtues, especially those which are tender and weak. The duty of keeping our good name, and being such as we are esteemed, powerfully yet gently presses us to a greathearted courage. Let us preserve our virtues, my dear Philothea, because they are pleasing to God, the great and sovereign object of all our action. Those who want to preserve fruits are not satisfied with covering them with sugar but put them in jars suitable for their preservation. In the same way, although divine love is the principal preservative of our virtues, we can still make use of our good name as very suitable and useful for that purpose.

However, we are not to be very eager, exacting and too formal in preserving our good name. For those who are very touchy and sensitive about their reputation resemble those who take medicines for every little discomfort. While thinking of preserving their health, they ruin it utterly. In the same manner, those who wish to keep their reputation with such concern lose it entirely.

Let us always fix our eyes on Jesus Christ crucified. Let us go forward in his service with confidence and simplicity, with wisdom and discretion. He will be the protector of our good name; if he allows it to be taken away from us, it will be either to give us a better one or to make us progress in holy humility of which one ounce is better than a thousand pounds of honor. If we are unjustly blamed, let us peacefully oppose calumny with the truth. If it lasts, let us continue to humble ourselves, thus entrusting our reputation and ourselves into the hands of God. We will never be able to secure it better.

(Introduction III, 7)

Gentleness

According to apostolic tradition the holy chrism used in God's Church for confirmation and consecrations is composed of olive oil mixed with balm. Among other things it represents the two favorite and beloved virtues which shone forth in the sacred person of our Lord. He has particularly recommended them to us to indicate that through them our hearts are to be specially consecrated to his service and dedicated to his imitation: *Learn of me,* he says, *for I am gentle and humble of heart* (Mt 11:29). Humility makes us perfect toward God and gentle toward our neighbor. The balm, which as I mentioned earlier always sinks lower than all other liquids, symbolizes gentleness; kindness, the flower of charity, rises above all things and is outstanding among virtues. According to St. Bernard charity reaches its perfection when it is not only patient but also gentle and meek.

Take care, Philothea, that this mystical chrism made up of gentleness and humility is within your heart. For it is one of the great tricks of the enemy to make many people satisfied with words and the external appearances of these two virtues. Those who do not examine well their interior dispositions imagine themselves to be humble and gentle though in practice they are not. We recognize them to be such because in spite of their ceremonious gentleness and humility, they burst out with unparalleled arrogance at the least offensive word or at the least insult they receive. It is said that those who have taken the preventive commonly known as the grace of St. Paul do not suffer from inflammations when bitten and stung by a viper provided the preventive is of excellent quality. So too when humility and gentleness are good and authentic we are guaranteed against the inflammations and passions which insults usually provoke in our hearts. When bitten and stung by detractors and enemies, if we become proud, puffed up and vexed, it is a sure sign that our humility and gentleness were not genuine and sincere but artificial and apparent.

The holy and illustrious patriarch Joseph, while sending his brothers from Egypt back to his father's house, gave them this one word of advice: *Do not become angry on the way* (Gn 45:24). I say the same to you Philothea: this miserable life is only a progressive journey to the happy life to come. Therefore let us not be angry at all with one another on the way. Let us walk in the company of our family and companions gently, peacefully and kindly. Further, I tell you very plainly and without any exception: do not become angry at all if that is possible. Do not accept any pretext whatever to open the door of your heart to anger. For St. James says bluntly and without reservation that human anger *does not work the justice of God* (Jas 1:20).

We ought, indeed, to resist the evil and restrain the vices of those in our charge constantly and courageously but gently and peacefully. Nothing calms down an angry elephant so quickly as the sight of a little lamb and nothing breaks the force of cannon-balls so easily as wool. We do not accept a correction given in anger, even though reasonable, as well as the one that has no other origin than reason alone. For the rational soul is naturally subject to reason and is subject to passion only through tyranny. Reason accompanied by passion becomes odious, its rightful dominion being degraded by its association with tyranny.

It is better to learn to live without anger than to try to make a wise and moderate use of anger. When we find ourselves surprised by it due to our imperfection or weakness, it is better to repel it promptly than to bargain with it. Even in the little delay offered to it, it makes itself mistress of the place, like the serpent which draws easily the whole of its body where it can put in its head. But you will ask: how can I repel it? You should, my dear Philothea, at the very first feeling of anger gather promptly all your strength, not too roughly or impetuously but gently and yet seriously. We often see, in the sessions of several senates and parliaments, that the ushers crying out "Silence" make more noise than those whom they want to silence. So too it happens many a time that, by trying to repress anger violently, we stir up more agitation in our hearts than anger itself would have done. The heart thus agitated can no longer be master of itself.

After this gentle effort, put into practice the advice given by St. Augustine in his old age to the young bishop Auxilius:

> Do what a person should do. If what the psalmist says happens to you: *My eye is troubled with great anger,* have recourse to God crying: *Have mercy on me Lord* (Ps 30:10), so that he may stretch his right hand to restrain your anger.

I mean that, when we see ourselves agitated by anger, we must implore the help of God, following the example of the apostles tossed about by the wind and the storm in the midst of the waters (Mt 8:24-26). For he will command our passions to be still and there will be a great calm. But I wish to make you aware that the prayer which is made against a present, pressing anger ought to be gentle, tranquil and not violent. This is to be followed in all the remedies we use against this evil.

Moreover, as soon as you perceive that you have acted with anger, make reparation for the fault by a prompt act of gentleness toward the same person against whom you were irritated. For just as the best remedy against lying is to disown it as soon as we become aware of it, in like manner, it is a good remedy against anger to correct it instantly through a contrary act of gentleness; as they say, fresh wounds are easily healed.

Besides, when you are at peace and without any anger, store up for yourself a supply of gentleness and kindness. Do this by saying all your words, doing all your actions, both small and great with the utmost gentleness possible.

(*Introduction* III, 8)

One of the excellent practices of gentleness that we could learn has to do with ourselves: never to be provoked at ourselves or our imperfections. Even though it is reasonable that we must be sorry and displeased when we commit some faults, yet we must refrain from a harsh, vexed gloomy and angry displeasure. Many make a great mistake in this regard. When they are overcome by anger, they become angry at being angry, vexed at being vexed, fretful at being fretful. By this means, they keep their hearts steeped and soaked in anger. Although it may seem that the second anger destroys the first, it actually serves as an opening and a passage for fresh anger at the first occasion which presents itself. Moreover, these vexations, harshness and anger which we have against ourselves tend to pride. They have no other origin than self-love which is disturbed and anxious at seeing ourselves imperfect.

Believe me, Philothea, the correction made by a father gently and with love has much more power to correct the child than one made with anger and fury. So too when our heart has committed some fault, we must correct it with gentle, calm remonstrances, with more compassion for it than anger against it, encouraging it to amendment. Thus the repentance it will form will sink in much more and penetrate more deeply than a fretful angry, stormy repentance.

As for myself, if I had, for example, taken great care not to fall into the vice of vanity and yet fell deeply into it, I would not like to correct my heart in the following manner: "Are you not wretched and abominable that after so many resolutions you allowed yourself to be carried away by vanity? Die of shame, do not raise your eyes to heaven, you blind, shameless traitor, disloyal to your God"; and similar expressions. But I would like to correct it reasonably by means of compassion: "Alas! my poor heart, here we are fallen again into the ditch which we have so firmly decided to avoid. Let us get up and leave it for ever. Let us entreat the mercy of God and hope that henceforth it will help us to be firm; let us return to the path of humility. Courage; henceforth let us be on our guard. God will help us and we shall do better." I would like to build up a firm and solid resolution never to fall into the same fault taking suitable means for this and following likewise the opinion of my spiritual director.

Raise your heart, then, whenever it falls, very gently humbling yourself profoundly before God for the knowledge of your misery. Do not be in the least surprised at your fall since it is not astonishing that infirmity is infirm, weakness is weak and misery is wretched. Nevertheless, detest with all your strength the offence God has received from you. With great courage and confidence in his mercy, put yourself back on the path of virtue which you had forsaken.

(Introduction III, 9)

Virtues Needed for Living in the Midst of Things

Care without Anxiety Concerning What One Has to Do

The care and diligence we should have in our affairs are quite different from solicitude, anxiety and eagerness. The angels are concerned about our salvation and they obtain it with diligence but they do not have solicitude, anxiety or eagerness. Care and diligence flow from their charity, but solicitude, anxiety and eagerness would be entirely contrary to their happiness. For care and diligence may be accompanied by peace and tranquility of spirit but not solicitude or anxiety and much less eagerness. Be careful and diligent, Philothea, in all your affairs of which you are in charge, since God who entrusted them to you desires that you take great care of them. But if it is possible, be not solicitous or anxious about them, that is, do not undertake them with restlessness, anxiety and eagerness. Do not be eager at work because every kind of eagerness disturbs reason and judgment. It even prevents us from doing well the very things of which we are too eager.

When our Lord corrects St. Martha he says: *Martha, Martha, you are worried and anxious about many things* (Lk 10:41). You see, if she had been simply careful, she would not have been troubled at all. As she was anxious and disturbed she was in a hurry and was troubled. It is about this that our Lord corrects her. The rivers flowing gently through the plains carry along large boats and rich merchandise. Rains falling gently on fields make them plentiful in grass and grain. But streams and rivers with strong currents rush through the land, ruin their neighborhood and are useless for navigation. Likewise heavy showers and tempests ravage fields and meadows.

Nothing done impulsively and in a hurry is ever well done. As the ancient proverb has it, we must expedite matters peacefully. *He who hurries up,* says Solomon, *runs the risk of stumbling and hurting his feet* (Prv 19:2). We always do fast enough when we do well. Drones make much more noise and are more in a hurry than the bees but they make only wax and no honey.[1] Thus those who rush around with tormenting anxiety and noisy solicitude do neither much nor well.

Flies do not trouble us by their strength but by their number. Accept your affairs in peace as they come and strive to do them in order, one after another. For if you wish to do them all at once or in disorder, the efforts you make will crush and exhaust your spirit. Thus you will remain usually overburdened, under pressure and ineffectual.

In all your affairs, rely entirely on the providence of God through which alone all your plans succeed. All the same, on your part strive very gently to cooperate with it. Then believe that if you trust well in God, success will come to you. It will be more useful for you, whether it seems good or bad to you according to your particular way of judging.

Do as little children who with one hand hold fast to the hand of their father and with the other gather strawberries or blackberries along the hedges. In the same manner, while gathering and managing the goods of this world with one hand, hold fast with the other to the hand of your heavenly Father, turning to him from time to time to see if your actions or occupations are pleasing to him. Take care, above all, that you do not leave his hand and protection thinking of collecting and gathering more. For if he abandons you, you would not take even a single step without falling flat on your face to the ground. I mean, Philothea, that amidst your ordinary affairs and occupations which do not require a strict and earnest attention, you look more at God than at your affairs. When what you have to do is so weighty that it requires all your attention to do it well, you will still look toward God from time to time, acting like sailors who, to reach the land they seek look more up to the sky than down where they are sailing. Thus God will work with you, in you and for you and your work will be followed by consolation.

(*Introduction* III, 10)

---

1. St. Francis shared the mistaken belief of his contemporaries that drones make wax.

Care without Anxiety Concerning What One Has

Happy are the poor in spirit for theirs is the kingdom of God (Mt 5:3). Accursed then are the rich in spirit for theirs is the misery of hell. Those are rich in spirit who have riches in their spirit or their spirit in riches. Those are poor in spirit who have neither riches in their spirit nor their spirit in riches. The halcyons make their nests round like a ball and leave only a small opening from the top. They put them on the seashore and yet they remain so strong and impenetrable that, even when washed by the waves, water never enters them. Thus always floating, they remain in the midst of the sea, on the sea and masters of the sea.[1] Your heart, Philothea, is to be like that, open only to heaven, impenetrable to riches and perishable things. If you have them, keep your heart free from attachment to them. Let it always remain above riches; and in the midst of riches, let it be without riches and master of riches. No, do not put this heavenly spirit within earthly goods. Let it always be their master, above them and not in them.

There is a difference between keeping poison and being poisoned. The pharmacists almost all keep poisons, to make use of them in different circumstances. But they are not for that matter poisoned because they do not have poison in their bodies but only in their shops. So too you can own riches without being poisoned by them. Such will be the case, if you have them in your house, or in your purse, and not in your heart.

Do not desire with a full and earnest longing the wealth you do not have. Do not fix your heart deeply on what you have. Do not be distressed at the losses sustained. Then you have some reason to believe that, being rich in reality, you are not rich in affection, but you are poor in spirit, and consequently blessed, *for the kingdom of heaven belongs to you* (Mt 5:3).

(*Introduction* III, 14)

Dear Philothea, I would like to put into your heart both riches and poverty together, a great care and a great indifference for temporal things. Have much greater care than the worldly people to make your wealth

---

1. The halcyon is a fabled bird, usually identified with a species of kingfisher. Cf. Pliny the Elder (A.D. 23-79), *Historia Naturalis* X. The ancients believed that it bred about the time of the winter solstice in a nest floating on the sea. It was able to charm the wind and waves so that the sea was especially calm during the period.

useful and profitable. Tell me, are not the gardeners of the great princes more careful and diligent in cultivating and beautifying the gardens they have in their charge than if they were their own? But why is this so? Certainly, they think of these gardens as the gardens of princes and kings. They like to make themselves acceptable to them by these services. Dear Philothea, the possessions which we have are not our own. God has given them to us to develop and wants us to make them profitable and useful and thus render him loving service in taking care of them. This care, then, ought to be greater and more dedicated than that which worldly people have for their possessions. For they are busy only for love of themselves but we must work for the love of God. As self-love is a violent, agitated, eager love, so too the care taken for it is full of trouble, vexation and anxiety. As the love of God is gentle, peaceful and tranquil, the care which proceeds from it, though it is for the good of the world, is kind, gentle and considerate.

Let us then have this considerate care for the preservation of our temporal goods, and even for their increase, when a just occasion presents itself and insofar as our situation demands it. For God wishes us to do so out of love for him. But take care that self-love does not deceive you, because sometimes it imitates the love of God so well that it would appear to be genuine. To prevent it from deceiving us and the care of temporal goods from degenerating into avarice, besides what I have said in the preceding chapter, we should often practice real and effectual poverty in the midst of all the possessions and riches God has given us.

Give up always a part of your resources by giving them to the poor with a generous heart. To give away what we possess is to impoverish ourselves by that much, and the more you give, the more you grow poor. It is true that God will give it back to you, not only in the next world but even in this. In fact, there is nothing which contributes more to temporal prosperity than almsgiving. But as you wait for God to restore it to you, till then you will be deprived of it. How holy and rich is the impoverishment brought about by almsgiving!

Love the poor and poverty because by this love you will become truly poor; as scripture says, we become like the things we love (Hos 9:10). Love makes the lovers equal: *Who is weak with whom I am not weak?* (2 Cor 11:29), says St. Paul. He could say: Who is poor with whom I am not poor? Indeed, love made him to be such as those whom he loved. If therefore you love the poor, you will certainly share their poverty and be poor like them. Now if you love the poor be often among them. Be happy to see them at your home and visit them at their homes. Talk with them willingly. Be quite at ease when they come near you in the church, in the streets and elsewhere. Be poor in the language you make use of. Speak to them like their companions but have generous hands giving them your gifts more in abundance.

Would you like to do still more, dear Philothea? Do not be satisfied with being poor like the poor, but be poorer than the poor. How is this possible? The *servant* is less than his *master* (Jn 13:16). Make yourself then the servant of the poor. Go to serve them in their beds when they are sick, and this with your own hands. Be their cook and at your own expense. Be their tailor and washerwoman. Dear Philothea, this service is more glorious than that of royalty.

I cannot admire enough the fervor with which this counsel was practiced by St. Louis, one of the great kings the world has seen, but I say a great king with every kind of greatness. Very often he served at the table of the poor whom he was maintaining. Almost every day he made three of them sit at his own table, and often ate the rest of their soup with an extraordinary love. When he visited the hospitals of the sick, which he did very often, he used to serve those who had the most loathsome diseases like the leprous, the ulcerous and others like them. He did them all this service bareheaded, kneeling on the ground, respecting in their persons the Savior of the world, and cherishing them with a love as tender as that of a gentle mother for her child. St. Elizabeth, daughter of the king of Hungary, usually mixed with the poor, and for recreation dressed like a poor woman among her ladies, telling them: "If I were poor I would dress like this." Dear Philothea, this prince and princess were indeed poor amidst their riches, and rich in their poverty.

Blessed are those who are thus poor, for the kingdom of heaven belongs to them (Mt 5:3). *I was hungry, you fed me. I was cold you clothed me. Possess the kingdom which has been prepared for you from the foundation of the world* (Mt 25:34-36). The King of the poor and of kings will say this at the great judgment.

There is no one who has not experienced at times some want or lack of convenience. Sometimes it happens that a guest comes to our house, whom we would like to and should treat well, but do not have the means at the moment. We have fine clothes in one place, but may need them in another where we are bound to appear in public. It happens that all the wines in our cellar ferment and turn sour, and there are left only wines that are of poor quality and immature. We find ourselves in the country in some hovel where everything is lacking: we have neither bed, nor room, nor table, nor service. In short, it is easy often to be in need of something, however rich we may be. This is being effectually poor with regard to what we lack. Philothea, be quite at ease on these occasions, accept them with a good heart, bear them cheerfully.

(*Introduction* III, 15)

If you are really poor, dearest Philothea, be such also in spirit. Make a virtue of necessity and make use of this precious stone of poverty for what it is worth. Its brilliance is not discovered in this world; nevertheless it is exceedingly beautiful and rich. Have patience, you are in good company: our Lord, our Lady, the apostles and so many men and women saints have been poor. Although capable of becoming rich, they disdained being so. How many well-placed people there are who with much opposition have undertaken a painstaking search to find holy poverty in cloisters or in hospitals? They exerted much effort to go find her—witness Saints Alexis, Paula, Paulinus, Angela and so many others—and look, Philothea, she comes to present herself to you, showing herself more gracious in your regard. You have met her without searching for her and without effort. Embrace her then as the dear friend of Jesus Christ who was born, lived and died in poverty, and who was nourished by her all his life.

Your poverty, Philothea, has two great privileges by means of which you are enabled to acquire great merit. The first is that poverty did not come to you by your choice but solely by the will of God who made you poor without the consent of your own will. What we receive simply from the will of God is always very pleasing to him, provided we receive it with a cheerful heart and love of his holy will. Where there is less of our will, there is more of God's will. Simple and absolute acceptance of God's will renders the suffering extremely pure.

The second privilege of this poverty is that it is a poverty that is truly poor. A poverty that is praised, caressed, esteemed, helped and assisted is allied to riches and at the least it is not poor at all. But a poverty that is despised, rejected, blamed, abandoned is truly poor. Such then is the poverty of the laity. Since they are not poor by their own choice but by necessity, it is not taken into much account. The poverty of the laity, not being held in great esteem, is poorer than that of the religious.

Do not be ashamed of being poor and of asking for alms in charity. Receive with humility what will be given to you and accept any refusal with gentleness. Often recall to mind the journey our Lady made to Egypt, to carry there her dear child. How much contempt, poverty and misery she had to endure! If you live like this, you will be very rich in your poverty.

(Introduction III, 16)

Virtues Needed for Living in the Midst of People

Being Alone and Being with Others

To seek the company of others and to shun it are two blameworthy extremes in the devotion of people living in society, which is the kind of devotion I am speaking about. To keep away from such company shows disdain and contempt of our neighbor and to search for it manifests idleness and aimlessness. We should love our neighbors as ourselves. To show that we love them we must not avoid being with them. To show that we love ourselves we ought to abide in ourselves when we are within ourselves. We are within ourselves when we are alone. Think of yourself, says St. Bernard, and then of others. Hence, if there is no urgent need for you to seek company or to receive someone at home, remain within yourself and reflect within your own heart; but, if company comes or some good reason invites you to be among people, go in the name of God, Philothea, and greet your neighbor willingly and graciously.

There are some social gatherings useless for anything else than recreation. These take place by mere change from serious occupations. Though we must not be addicted to them yet we can give them some time meant for relaxation.

Other social gatherings have courtesy as their purpose such as mutual visits and certain meetings for honoring the neighbor. We are not to be too scrupulous in attending them. So too we must not be impolite by holding them in contempt. But we must fulfill with moderation the duty we have so as to avoid equally rudeness and thoughtlessness.

There remain useful social gatherings such as those of devout and virtuous persons. Philothea, it will always be a great benefit for you to find such gatherings and to frequent them. The vine planted among olive trees bears oily grapes which have the taste of olives. A person who finds him or herself often in the company of virtuous people cannot but share their qualities. Drones alone are not able to make honey, but they help the bees to make it. It is of great help for us to associate with devout persons in order to progress in devotion.

Besides the mental solitude, to which you may turn in the midst of the greatest transactions,[1] you must always love the real solitude of a place. You need not go into the deserts like St. Mary of Egypt, St. Paul, St. Anthony, Arsenius and other solitaries. Instead remain in your room, in your garden, or elsewhere for a short while. There at will you may withdraw your spirit into your heart and refresh your mind by good reflections and holy thoughts, or by a short reading, following the example of the great Bishop Nazianzen. Speaking of himself he says:

> I walked alone with myself at sunset, or passed my time on the seashore. For I was accustomed to make use of this recreation to relax myself and to shake off a little of my usual worries.

Then he describes the good thoughts he had which I have mentioned elsewhere.[2] Again, we have the example of St. Ambrose. Speaking of him, St. Augustine[3] says that often on entering his room (no one was refused entrance), he saw him reading. After waiting for sometime, afraid of disturbing him, he used to turn back without saying a word. He thought that this little time which remained for this great pastor for strengthening and refreshing his spirit after the rush of so many affairs must not be taken away from him. Also after the apostles had on one day told our Lord how they had preached and worked hard, he told them: *Come to the solitude and rest there for a while* (Mk 6:31).

(*Introduction* III, 24)

---

1. Part II, chapter 12.
2. Part II, chapter 13.
3. *Confessions* VI, 3.

Advice on Conversation

"Someone who does not trip up in speech," says St. James, "has reached perfection" (Jas 3:2). Take great care that you do not let slip any unbecoming words from your lips. Even though you may not say them with an evil intention, those who hear them may take them in a different way. An unbecoming word which falls into a feeble heart spreads and extends like a drop of oil on a piece of cloth. Sometimes it seizes the heart in such a way as to fill it with a thousand impure thoughts and temptations. Just as what poisons the body enters through the mouth, so too what poisons the heart enters through the ear. The tongue which produces it is murderous. Sometimes, by chance, the poison ejected by the tongue does not produce any effect because the heart of the hearers happens to be strengthened by some antidote. True, in such cases the poison does not cause their death, but it is not due to the lack of the malice of the one who speaks.

Let no one tell me that he intends no evil, for our Lord, who knows human intentions, has said that *the mouth speaks from the abundance of the heart* (Mt 12:34). Even if we intend no evil, the evil one does, and he always uses these evil words insidiously to pierce another's heart. It is said that those who have eaten the herb called angelica[1] always have a pleasant and agreeable breath. Those who have the angelic virtue of modesty and chastity in their hearts always speak pure, polite and suitable words. As to indecent and foolish things, the apostle wants us not even to name them (Eph 5:3). He assures us that nothing *corrupts good manners* so much as *evil exchanges* (1 Cor 15:33).

As to words spoken in fun among ourselves with a modest gaiety and joyfulness, they belong to the virtue which is called *eutrapelia* by the Greeks, which we may term pleasant conversation. By them, we take a decent and friendly recreation from trifling situations which human imperfections cause. However, we must guard against passing from this simple joyfulness to mockery. Mockery provokes laughter through the contempt and scorn of our neighbor. But gaiety and humor cause laughter through simple freedom, trust, familiar simplicity joined to the charm of some words.

(*Introduction* III, 27)

---

1. Aromatic plant used in cooking.

Do not judge that you will not be judged, says our Savior; *do not condemn and you will not be condemned* (Lk 6:37). *No,* says the apostle, *do not judge before the time till the Lord who will reveal the secrets of darkness and will manifest the counsels of the hearts comes* (1 Cor 4:5). How displeasing to God are rash judgments!

The judgments of human beings are rash because they are not judges of one another. In judging they take over the function of our Lord. They are rash because the principal malice of sin depends on the intention and *consent of the heart* which is a *secret hidden in darkness* for us. They are rash because each one has enough to do in judging oneself without attempting to judge one's neighbor. So that we ourselves may not be judged, we should not judge others but judge ourselves. While our Lord forbids the one, the apostle commands the other, saying: *If we judge ourselves, we will not be judged* (1 Cor 11:31). But, my God, we do exactly the opposite. Indeed, we do not stop doing what is forbidden to us by judging our neighbor at every turn, and never do what is enjoined on us—to judge ourselves.

We must remedy rash judgments starting with the causes of their origin. There are some hearts which are harsh, bitter and hard by their nature. They convey the same harshness and bitterness to everything they receive. Thus they convert *judgment into wormwood* as the prophet says (Am 6:13), by never judging others except with extreme severity and harshness. They are in great need of being treated by a good spiritual physician. It is difficult to overcome this bitterness of heart since it is natural to them. Although it is not a sin in itself but an imperfection, yet it is quite dangerous because it introduces rash judgments and slander into the heart and make them reign there. Some judge rashly not from bitterness but from pride, thinking that according to the measure in which they lower the honor of another, they raise their own. Being arrogant and presumptuous persons, they admire themselves and place themselves very high in their own esteem. Hence they look down on all the others as mean and low: *I am not like the rest,* said the foolish Pharisee (Lk 18:11).

Others judge according to their emotions. They always think well of what they love, and always ill of what they hate. An exception is the astonishing yet real case in which excess of love arouses them to judge badly what they love. This is a monstrous effect which comes also from an impure, imperfect, troubled and sick love which is jealousy. As everyone knows, it condemns persons loved as guilty of infidelity and adultery for a simple look or for the least smile in the world. Finally, fear, ambition and such weakness of the mind often contribute very much to cause suspicion and rash judgment.

But what are the remedies? Those who drink the juice of the herb called *ophiusa* of Ethiopia imagine that they see everywhere serpents and terrifying things.[1] Those who have swallowed pride, envy, ambition, hatred see nothing which they do not find evil or discreditable. The former must take the palm wine in order to be cured. I suggest the same kind of remedy for the latter. Drink as much as you can of the sacred wine of charity. It will free you from these evil moods which cause you to make distorted judgments. Charity is afraid of meeting evil, so far is it from going in search of it. When charity meets with evil, it turns away from it and takes no notice of it. It even closes its eyes before seeing it at the first rumor of evil it hears. Then it believes by a holy simplicity that it was not evil but some shade or phantom of evil. If, by force, it recognizes that it is evil itself, it turns away from it immediately and tries to forget its form. Charity is the great remedy for all evils but particularly for rash judgments.

(*Introduction* III, 28)

In your speech be gentle, free, sincere, straightforward, simple and truthful. Be on your guard against duplicity, cunning and pretence. Although it is not good to say always all kinds of truths, yet it is never allowed to go against truth. Accustom yourself never to tell a lie deliberately either by way of excuse or for any other reason. Remember that God is the *God of truth* (Ps 31:5). If you happen to tell a lie inadvertently and you can correct it on the spot, by some explanation or alteration, do so. A genuine apology is a more gracious and effective excuse than any lie.

Although we may sometimes discreetly and prudently disguise and conceal the truth by some play on words, yet it is not to be done except in a matter of importance when the glory and service of God clearly requires it. Beyond this such tricks of words are dangerous. For as scripture says *the holy Spirit* does not abide in a *deceitful* and double-dealing person (Wis 1:5). There is no ingenuity so good and desirable as

---

1. Pliny the Elder, *Historia Naturalis*, XXIV. The name of the herb comes from the Greek word *ophis*, serpent.

simplicity. Worldly prudence and carnal devices belong to the children of this world. But the children of God walk sincerely with an open heart. *Whoever walks with simplicity,* says the sage, *walks confidently* (Prv 10:9). Lying, duplicity and pretence always manifest a weak and mean spirit.

St. Augustine had said in the fourth book of his *Confessions*[1] that his soul and that of his friend were just one soul. After the death of his friend, this life was dreadful for him because he did not wish to live by halves. For that same reason, he was afraid of dying by chance lest his friend should die completely. Later these words seemed to him very artificial and exaggerated so that he revoked them in the book of his *Retractions.* He called them an absurdity. Do you see, dear Philothea, how this beautiful person was sensitive to the feelings of artificiality in words? Indeed, truthfulness, simplicity and sincerity in speech are a great ornament to Christian life.

(Introduction III, 30)

We are human only through our reason. Yet it is a rare thing to find people truly reasonable. Especially since self-love generally confuses reason, it leads us unnoticeably into a thousand kinds of small but dangerous injustices and unfair dealings. These, like the *little foxes* spoken of in the Song of Songs *destroy the vines* (Sg 2:15). As they are small we do not pay attention to them. Because they are many, they do not cease to do much harm.

I shall now point out to you certain unfair and unreasonable attitudes. We accuse our neighbor for a little and we excuse ourselves much. We wish to sell very dear and buy quite cheap. We desire that justice be done in the house of another and at home we show mercy and indulgence to our own. We want our words to be taken in a good sense by others and we are touchy and sensitive to what others say. We would like our neighbor to leave us his property when we pay him. Is it not more just that he keeps it and leave us our money? We are displeased with him because he does not want to adjust to us. Has he not greater reason to be angry with us because we wish to inconvenience him? If we are attached to a particular practice, we despise all the rest and criticize all that is not according to our taste.

---

1. Chapter 6.

Philothea, be impartial and just in your actions. Put yourself always in the place of your neighbor, and your neighbor in your own place, and thus you will judge him or her well. Make yourself a seller while buying and a buyer while selling, and you will sell and buy with justice. All these acts of justice are small and do not oblige us to restitution since we remain strictly within the limits of what is advantageous to us. But they continue to oblige us to correct our attitudes because these are great defects of reason and charity. After all these are simply deceits. We lose nothing by living generously, nobly, courteously and with a magnanimous, impartial and reasonable heart. Remember, then, dear Philothea, to examine your heart often to see if it is disposed toward your neighbor as you would like your neighbor's heart disposed toward you. For this is the mark of true reason.

(*Introduction* III, 36)

Friendship

Love holds the first rank among the emotions of the soul. It is the king of all the movements of the heart. Love changes all the rest to itself and makes us such as what is loved. Be on your guard then, dear Philothea, that there is no evil whatever in your love, because if there is, soon you will become completely evil. For friendship is the most dangerous love of all. While other loves can be had without communication, friendship— which is entirely based on communication—can scarcely be had without participating in the friend's qualities.

All love is not friendship because:

1. We can love without being loved. In this case there is love but not friendship, insofar as friendship is a mutual love. If it is not mutual, it is not friendship.
2. It is not enough that it is mutual; the persons who love each other ought to know their reciprocal affection because, if they do not know it, they will have love but not friendship.
3. Between them, there must also be some kind of communication, which is the basis of friendship.

According to the variety of communications, friendships will vary. The communications are different depending on the difference of the things we communicate to each other. If these are false and vain, the friendship is false and vain. If they are genuine, the friendship is genuine. The more excellent the good things communicated, the more excellent will be the friendship. Just as honey is of the best quality if taken from the most exquisite flowers, so too love based on a most exquisite communication is the most excellent.

(*Introduction* III, 17)

Philothea, love everyone with a great love of charity, but have friendship with those capable of communicating virtuous things to you. The more exquisite the virtue you put in your exchanges, the more perfect will your friendship be. If you share knowledge, your friendship is indeed very praiseworthy; more so if you communicate virtues, prudence, discretion, fortitude and justice. If your mutual and reciprocal exchange is about charity, devotion, Christian perfection, precious indeed will your friendship be. It will be excellent because it comes from God, excellent because it tends to God, excellent because its bond is God, excellent because it will last eternally in God. How good it is to love on earth as one loves in heaven, and to learn to cherish one another in this world as we shall do eternally in the next!

I do not speak here about the simple love of charity for it ought to embrace all people. But I speak of the spiritual friendship by which two or three or more persons communicate among themselves their devotion, their spiritual affection and become one in spirit. With good reason such happy souls can sing: *How good and pleasant it is for kindred to dwell together* (Ps 133:1). Yes, this delicious balm of devotion distills from one heart to another, by a continual sharing, so that we may say that *God has poured out his blessing and life* on this friendship for ever and ever (Ps 133:3).

In my opinion, all other friendships are only shadows compared to this. Their bonds are only chains of glass and jet[1] in comparison with this great bond of holy devotion which is entirely of gold. Do not form friendships of any other kind—I mean friendships which you make. On account of this, you are not to abandon or disregard the friendships which nature and earlier duties oblige you to cultivate toward relations, associates, benefactors, neighbors and others. I now speak of those friendships which you yourself choose.

---

1. A hard black mineral used for ornaments.

Perhaps many people may tell you that you should not have any kind of special affection and friendship since it occupies the heart, distracts the mind and creates jealousies. But they err in their advice. For they have found in the writings of many saints and devout authors that particular friendships and excessive affections do very great harm to religious. They think that in itself it is the same for all other persons. But there is a big difference.

In a well-ordered monastery, the common purpose of all tends toward true devotion, so it is not necessary to have private sharing there, lest by seeking in private what is in common, they would pass from particularity to partiality.

But it is necessary that those who live in the world and embrace true devotion join together in a holy and sacred friendship. By this means they encourage, assist and support one another for their mutual good.

Just as those who walk on level ground do not need a helping hand, but those who are on a dangerous and slippery path support one another to walk more safely, so too those who are religious do not need particular friendships. But those who are in the world do need them, to save themselves and help one another in the midst of so many difficult paths they have to cross. In the world, all do not strive for the same end, all do not have the same spirit. Hence, without doubt, it is necessary to draw oneself aside and form friendships according to our aim. This particularity is indeed a partiality, but a holy partiality which does not cause any division except between good and evil, between sheep and goats, and between bees and hornets—a necessary separation.

(Introduction III, 19)

Letters of Spiritual Friendship

To Madame de Chantal

What difference does it make if you know whether or not you can consider me your spiritual father, as long as you know how my soul is disposed toward yours, and I know how yours is toward mine? I know you have complete confidence in my affection; I have no doubt about this and delight in the thought. I want you to know and to believe that I have an intense and very special desire to serve you with all my strength. It would be impossible for me to explain either the quality or the greatness of this desire that I have to be at your spiritual service, but I can tell you that I believe it is from God, and for that reason, I cherish it and every day see it growing and increasing remarkably. If it were appropriate, I would say more, and say it in all truth, but I had better stop here. Dear Madam, you can see clearly enough to what extent you may call on me and trust me. Make the most of my affection and of all that God has given me for the service of your soul. I am all yours; give no more thought to the role or to the rank I hold in being yours. God has given me to you; so consider me as yours in him, and call me whatever you like; it makes no difference.

Further, in order to cut short all the rebuttals which may be taking shape in your mind, I must tell you that I have never understood that there was any bond between us carrying with it any obligation but that of charity and true Christian friendship, what St. Paul calls *the bond of perfection* (Col 3:14);[1] and truly, that is just what it is, for it is indissoluble and never weakens. All other bonds are temporal, even that of a vow of obedience which can be broken through death or other circumstances; but the bond of love grows and gets ever stronger with time. It cannot be cut down by death, which, like a scythe, mows down everything but charity. *Love is strong as death and firm as hell* (cf. Sg 8:6), says Solomon. So there, dear sister (allow me to call you by this name, which is the one used by the apostles and the first Christians to express the intimate love they had for one another), this is our bond, these are our chains which, the more they are tightened and press against us, the more they bring us joy and freedom. Their strength is gentleness; their violence, mildness; nothing is more pliable than that; nothing stronger. Think of me as very closely bound to you, and don't try to understand more about it than that this bond is not opposed to any other bond either of a vow or of marriage. Be totally at peace on that score.

(*Letters*, pp. 126-28)

So we'll be all right, dear daughter, with God's help. All the little complications and hidden contradictions that come up unexpectedly to disturb my peace actually fill me with an even more serene peace and, it seems to me, are a sign that my soul will soon be settled in God. This really is the greatest and, I believe, the only ambition and passion of my heart. When I say my heart I mean my whole heart, including the person to whom God has united me indissolubly.

---

1. Following the Vulgate: *vinculum perfectionis.*

While I am on the subject of my soul, I want to give you some good news about it: I am doing and shall continue doing for it all that you asked me to do—have no doubt about this. Thank you for your concern for its welfare, which is undivided from the welfare of your own soul (if we can even use the terms "yours" and "mine" when speaking on this subject). And I'll tell you something else: I am a little happier than usual with my soul in that I no longer see anything in it which keeps it attached to this world, and I find it more in tune with eternal values. How happy I should be if I were as deeply and closely united to God as I am distanced and alienated from the world! And how delighted you would be, my daughter! But I'm speaking of my inner dispositions and my feelings; as for the exterior and, what is worse, my actions, these are full of all kinds of contrary flaws, for *I fail to carry out the good things I want to do* (Rom 7:15). Yet I know very well, without pretense and without swerving, that I really want to do them. But, my daughter, how can it be that even with such good will I still see so many imperfections growing in me? Surely, these come neither from my will nor by my will, although they appear to form part of it. It seems to me that they are like mistletoe which grows and appears on a tree though it is not part of it—on it but not of it. Why am I telling you all this? It's because my heart always expands and pours itself out spontaneously when it is near yours.

(*Letters*, pp. 150-51)

To Madame de Villesavin

Don't ever believe, my dearest daughter, that great distances can separate those whom God has united by the bonds of his love. The children of this world are all separated one from another because their hearts are in different places; but the children of God whose hearts are where their treasure is and who all have the same treasure—which is the same God—are consequently always bound and united together. In light of this, it shouldn't matter to us that necessity keeps you out of town and that very soon I will have to leave town to return to my duties. We shall often meet before our blessed crucifix if we observe carefully the promises we have made to each other; it is only there that our conversations are worthwhile.

(*Letters*, p. 178)

PART TWO

LOVE
FOR GOD

In Prayer

Prayer, a Heart to Heart with God

We express our love for God chiefly in two ways—spontaneously (affectively), and deliberately (effectively; or, as St. Bernard puts it, actively). In the first of these ways we grow fond of God, of what he likes; in the second we serve God, do what he enjoins. The first way unites us with God's goodness, the second urges us to carry out his will. The first way gives us our fill of gratification, of benevolence, of spiritual yearnings, desires, aspirations, fervor, leading us to commune heart to heart with God; the second way brings to birth in us the firm resolve, steadfast courage and absolute obedience necessary for carrying out whatever God's will ordains, also for suffering, accepting, approving, welcoming all that he permits. In the first we find God pleasing, in the second he is pleased with us; by the first we become pregnant with virtue, through the second we give birth to it; in the first way we clasp God to our hearts in loving embrace, in the second we carry him in our arms by the practice of virtue (cf. Sg 8:6).

We love God, in the first of these ways, principally by prayer. So many internal impulses are involved in this, it is impossible to put them all into words; not only because of their number, but also on account of their nature, their characteristics—being spiritual, they are inevitably subtle, almost beyond the reach of the human mind. Often the cleverest, best-trained hounds are put off the scent by the cunning of stags, which double back on their tracks or use their wiles to escape the pack. Just as frequently we lose our way when it comes to our emotions; they twist and turn so deftly, so unexpectedly, we cannot keep track of them.

God alone, through his infinite knowledge, can know, fathom and see through the ins and outs of the human mind. He reads our *thoughts from far away* (cf. Ps 138:3-5), he keeps track of all our twists and turns; such wonderful wisdom is far beyond our reach, no thoughts of ours can attain it. Most assuredly, to turn the mind in upon itself by introspection, by reflection, would be to enter a maze out of which we should almost certainly never find our way. To think of what we are thinking, to reflect on our reflections, to be conscious of our spiritual insights, to know that we are knowing, to remember that we are remembering—all this would demand an attention we cannot give, would so entangle us that we should find it impossible to break free. That is why this is a difficult book, especially for one who is not deeply prayerful.

I am not taking the word "prayer," in this context, merely in the sense of "petition" or "the request for some benefit which the faithful express in God's presence," as St. Basil describes it. I mean what St. Bonaventure meant when he said that prayer, widely speaking, embraces the whole of contemplative activity; what St. Gregory of Nyssa meant when he taught that "prayer is an interview or conversation between the soul and God"; also what St. Chrysostom had in mind when he asserted that "prayer is talking to God"; and finally, what St. Augustine and St. Damascene meant when they said that prayer is "an ascent, or uplifting of the mind toward God." If prayer is a talk or conversation between the soul and God, then in prayer we talk to God and God also speaks to us, we aspire to him and he inspires us, we are alive to him and he lives in us.

But what do we talk about in prayer? What is our topic of conversation? God, Theotimus; nothing else. After all, what does a lover talk about but his beloved? Prayer and mystical theology, therefore, are identical. Prayer is called theology, because it deals with God as speculative theology does; only there are three differences. First of all, speculative theology deals with God as the supreme being—the divinity of the supreme goodness; mystical theology deals with him as supremely lovable—the supreme goodness of the divinity. Secondly, speculative theology is concerned with God and the human being, mystical theology with God alone. Thirdly, speculative theology leads to knowledge of God—turning its pupils into learned scholars and theologians; mystical theology leads to love of God—turning out intensely affectionate lovers.

Prayer is called mystical, because of the hidden nature of the conversation: God and the individual speak heart to heart, and what passes between them can be shared with no one else. So personal is lovers' talk, it has no meaning outside the two who engage in it. "I lie asleep," said the mystic bride, "but oh, my heart is wakeful! (Sg 5:2). That is because *my true love's voice* is calling me." Who would have guessed it?—a sleeping bride, yet all the while deep in conversation with her bridegroom. No need, however, in the realms of love, for the spoken word, for appeal to the senses, when lovers share their thoughts. After all, prayer, or mystical theology, is simply a loving talk between the soul and God, where the topic of conversation is the attraction of God's goodness and how to achieve union with him.

Love craves privacy; even when lovers have no secrets to keep, they still prefer to talk in private. For one thing, if I am not mistaken, they feel that intimacy is lost when their conversation can be overheard; for another, their love for each other invests even ordinary topics with a new meaning, a different atmosphere. Although the language of love consists of a vocabulary in common use, its intonation is so personal as to be intelligible to no one but the lovers themselves. A friend's name spoken in public has no special significance; murmured intimately, in private, it is charged with wonder—the greater the intimacy, the more delightful it sounds. What a different language they speak, those ancient lovers of God—Ignatius, Cyprian, Chrysostom, Augustine, Hilary, Ephrem, Gregory, Bernard—from theologians whose love for God is not so great! We use the same words as they did: coming from them, however, those words held warmth and charm; coming from us, they are cold and stilted.

Love is not limited to lips alone for its expression; eyes, facial movements, sighs also have a part to play; even silence and reserve can deputize for words. *True to my heart's promise, I have eyes only for thee; I long, Lord, for thy presence* (Ps 26:8). *Keeping watch for the fulfillment of thy promise, my eyes languish for comfort still delayed* (Ps 118:82). *Listen, Lord, to my prayer, let my cry reach thy hearing, and my tears win answer* (Ps 38:13). *Day and night, Sion, let thy tears stream down,* cried out to Jerusalem the distressed hearts of its inhabitants; *never rest thou, never let that eye weary of its task* (Lam 2:18). The silence of saddened lovers was vocal through tearfilled eyes. Obviously the chief activity of mystical theology is to talk to God, and to listen to him as he speaks deep down in the heart. Since this dialogue consists of hidden aspirations and inspirations, we call it silent speech. Eyes speak to eyes, heart to heart, and none but those blessed lovers understands what passes between them.

(*Treatise* VI, 1)

Meditation, the First Step in Prayer

Meditation means thought, but thinking is not always meditating. There are times when the mind harbors thoughts for no rhyme or reason but to pass the time—like idle flies among the flowers. That kind of thing, however intent, cannot be called meditation; it is simply thought. Sometimes we think about something intently in order to learn its causes, effects, characteristics; such thought is called study—the mind acts like insects feeding indiscriminately on flowers and leaves. But when we think of divine things, to grow not in knowledge but in love . . . that is called meditation. We are meditating, when the mind does not trifle like flies, nor devour like insects, but wanders as a mystic bee here and there among the mysteries of God, to gather the honey of divine love.

So people are often preoccupied, harboring useless thoughts in their minds, practically unaware of what they are thinking about. Strangely enough, they are but inadvertently intent upon their thoughts; they would rather be without them—witness that man who said: *My mind is distracted with whirling thoughts* (Jb 17:11). People study too, laboriously filling themselves with useless knowledge, unable to resist inquisitiveness. Few people, however, devote themselves to meditating, to exciting a love for God in their hearts.

What it comes to is this: thinking and studying center round all kinds of things; but meditation, in the way I am using the word here, has to do with those things only that will make us good, devoted to God, if we reflect on them. So that meditation is simply a thought that we welcome again and again, that we harbor intently in our minds, in order to prompt our wills to give way to emotions which are holy or to make resolutions which are good.

Here and there among the flowers flies the bee in the springtime; not at random, but of set purpose; not for sheer delight in the gay flowered pattern of the countryside, but in search of honey. When it has found some, it sucks it in and carries it off to the hive, where it sets skillfully to work on it, separating the wax to form a comb in which to keep the honey for the following winter. It is the same with a devoted soul in meditation. From mystery to mystery it goes, never at haphazard or to gain comfort from seeing the wondrous beauty of divine things, but with the intention and purpose of discovering motives for loving God, for practicing virtue. These it embraces, when it has found them, enjoying them, locking them within its heart, where it sets apart what it feels will conduce to its progress, and ultimately forms suitable resolutions against time of temptation.

(*Treatise* VI, 2)

Contemplation and How it Differs
from Meditation

Contemplation, Theotimus, is but a loving, artless, unremitting, mental preoccupation with the things of God. You will see what I mean more easily, if I compare it with meditation.

The pupae of bees are called nymphs up to the time when they make honey; then they are called bees. In the same way prayer is called meditation until it succeeds in producing the honey of devotion; after that it is transformed into contemplation. Just as bees roam the countryside, pilfering nectar here and there among the flowers, busily engaged on what they gather, because they enjoy its sweetness . . . so we meditate to win God's love, after which we contemplate him, intent on his goodness, because love renders it sweet to us. Our longing to gain God's love causes us to meditate; love, when gained, leads to contemplation. Love renders the charm of what we love so pleasing, our minds never tire of reflecting on it.

We set out on the path of prayer by reflecting on God's goodness in order to prompt our wills to love him; but once love is conceived in our hearts, we continue our reflections on that goodness so as to gratify our love—and only constant sight of what we love can appease us.

It comes to this: when love is wedded to meditation, it gives birth to contemplation; we meditate to awaken love, we contemplate because we love. That is why I have described contemplation as a *loving* preoccupation—it is a child of love, and children always take their father's name.

(*Treatise* VI, 3)

Which is stronger, can you tell me: love in turning our gaze toward God, or sight in turning our hearts? Love demands knowledge, for we can never love the unknown; the more thorough does our knowledge of something good become, the deeper grows our love for it—as long as the emotion meets with no impediment. Still, it often happens that love, due to knowledge, does not keep pace with what the mind perceives, but spurts well on ahead. In this life, then, our love for God can exceed our knowledge of him. Hence St. Thomas's assertion[1] that women and

---

1. *Summa* 2. 2. q. 82. a. 3. ad 3.

childlike souls excel in devotion, more capable as a rule of loving God than are university professors and artists.

To your way of thinking, Theotimus, which of these two persons would have the greater love for light: someone blind from birth, who knew all that scientists have said in explanation and praise of it; or a field worker with keen eyes, who sees and enjoys the beauty of the rising sun? The blind man knows more about it, but the worker enjoys it more; and that enjoyment begets a much more passionate, intense love than ever mere intellectual knowledge can do—experiencing something good is vastly more enjoyable than knowing all the scientific facts about it. Our love for God starts with knowledge that faith gives of his goodness, a goodness we go on to experience and enjoy through love; love whets our appetite, but appetite increases our love. Just as we see waves, lashed by the wind, rolling and surging ever higher, each striving to outdo the next, so our taste for what is good enhances our love for it, and our love stimulates our taste. As the book of God's wisdom puts it: *Eat of this fruit, and you will yet hunger for more; drink of this wine, and your thirst for it is still unquenched* (Sir 24:29). Who loved God more, I ask you: the theologian Occam, from time to time described as the most subtle of mortals; or St. Catherine of Genoa, an unschooled woman? His knowledge of God was mostly from books, hers only from experience; yet her experience led her to the heights of seraphic love, while he—for all his learning—remained a stranger to such perfect bliss.

(*Treatise* VI, 4)

Meditation is a reflection in great detail, point by point, on those things which are capable of touching our hearts; contemplation, however, takes a single concentrated look at what we love—a concentrated reflection that has greater energy, greater power to move the will. There are two ways of admiring the beauty of a costly crown: either you can look at each of its jewels and precious stones in succession; or, after noting all the different pieces, you can take in the whole brilliant workmanship at a glance. The first way resembles meditation—when we reflect, for instance, on the expressions of God's mercy in order to quicken our love for him; but the second way is similar to contemplation—when we reflect, with one fixed gaze of the mind, on the diversity of those expressions as though we were looking at a single object of beauty. In meditation we tell over to ourselves, as it were, each of God's several perfections which we see in any given mystery; but in contemplation we add them all together and view them as one.

Meditation is like smelling first a carnation, then a rose, then rosemary, thyme, jasmine, orange-flower, each one separately; contemplation is equivalent to smelling the scented liquid distilled from all those flowers put together. Undoubtedly the combined scents in the liquid are sweeter, finer, than the separate scents of each flower. That is why the heavenly bridegroom sets such store by the fact that his true love looks at him *with one glance of an eye,* that her hair was dressed so as to give the impression of *one ringlet straying on* her *neck* (Sg 4:9). One glance simply implies a single concentrated gaze, without looking again and again; and one ringlet indicates a single idea undivided by various reflections.

(*Treatise* VI, 5)

Contemplation has this to be said for it: it is a pleasing occupation. It presumes that we have found God and his holy love, that we possess and enjoy him, saying: *I found him, so tenderly loved; and now that he is mine I will never leave him, never let him go* (Sg 3:4). That is how it differs from meditation, which is nearly always difficult, tiring, demanding a great deal of thought, as the mind makes its way from reflection to reflection in widespread search of its love's beloved or its beloved's love.

Meditation is like Jacob working to win Rachel; contemplation resembles his longed-for possession of her, all his work forgotten (cf. Gn 29:18).

In the mysteries of God, where the secrets of all other mysteries are to be found, lovers may eat their fill and sweethearts drink deep. People at a dinner, who eat more than they drink, remain sober; those who drink more than they eat become intoxicated. Meditation is a kind of eating: we chew over spiritual food with the teeth of reflection, to break it down, digest it; and this puts us to some trouble. Contemplation, on the other hand, is a kind of drinking: it is easy and natural, pleasant and smooth; but contemplation that is frequent and fervent, that takes one out of self to God, has an intoxicating effect. Blessed intoxication!—unlike drinking too much wine, it leaves us physically, not spiritually senseless; it does not stupefy or brutalize, but renders us angelic and, as it were, deifies us;

it takes us out of ourselves, not to abase us to the level of beasts, but to lift us above ourselves, set us with the angels; and it does this to make us more alive to God than to ourselves, lovingly intent on the vision of his beauty, lovingly bent on union with his goodness.

Normally, we can achieve contemplation only through hearing the word of God, discussing the spiritual life with others (like hermits of old), reading spiritual books, praying, meditating, singing hymns, thinking good thoughts. For this reason, doing such things amounts to contemplating, and those engaged in these activities are called contemplatives. Such a pursuit goes by the name of a contemplative life, on account of the activity of our minds—gazing at the truth of God's beauty and goodness with loving attentiveness; in other words, a love which makes us attentive, or an attentiveness resulting from, and adding to, the love we have for our Lord's infinite charms.

(*Treatise* VI, 6)

The Loving Recollection of a Soul Resting in God

By recollection, in this context, Theotimus, I do not mean the effort to be aware of God's presence, which people make at the beginning of their prayers, when they rein in their souls (so to speak), to have a heartfelt talk with God. That sort of recollection takes place at love's bidding; love it is which prompts us to pray, which inspires us to take this means of doing it well; so that such mental seclusion is our own doing.

No, the recollection I intend to describe here is not performed at love's bidding, but by love itself. In other words, it is not a question of our own choice; it is not ours to enjoy when we will, nor does it depend on our own efforts; it is all God's doing, grace working as he wills. To quote the saintly Mother Teresa of Jesus:[1]

> The author who wrote that recollection in prayer resembles a hedgehog rolling itself into a ball, or a tortoise withdrawing into its shell, made a telling comparison. But there is one big difference: those animals react in that way on their own initiative; we

---

1. Teresa of Avila, *Interior Castle,* mansion 4. 3.

have no control over recollection—it comes, not when we want
it, but when God sees fit to give us the grace.

It happens in this way. Nothing is more calculated than goodness to
attract, to unite to itself, such things as are conscious of it—our souls, for
example, which reach out for, or yield themselves to what they set great
store by, what they love. Occasionally, therefore, our Lord imperceptibly
infuses the sweetness of his charm into the depths of the soul, as an earnest
of his presence there. At this, the soul's powers, even its external senses,
impelled by some mysterious gratification, turn in upon that innermost
privacy where the beloved bridegroom waits.

Just as a freshly formed swarm of bees, poised for flight in search of
pastures new, can be recalled by the sound of gently clinking metal, or
by the scent of honeyed wine or sweet-smelling herbs and, while held by
the bait, made to enter the hive prepared for it; so our Lord, by uttering
some mysterious expression of love, or by the scented wine of his
affection more delicious than honey, or by *the perfume of his garments*
(Sg 4:11) (the caress of heaven upon our hearts) makes his loving
presence felt, attracting all the soul's faculties to muster round him, to
rest in him as the goal of their desire. If you were to put a piece of lodestone
in the center of a group of needles, you would see them all point
immediately in the direction of the magnet, and stick to it; so, when our
Lord makes his presence felt in the very core of the soul, all our faculties
turn in that direction, eager for union with a loving-kindness beyond
compare.

But I want you to take careful note of this: it is love, and love alone,
which is responsible for all that recollection. Love, aware of the beloved's
presence through his heart-felt attractions, pulls the soul together, turns
it in on him. All its faculties are delightfully withdrawn, gently turned and
lovingly directed toward the beloved, irresistibly attracted by those
charms he uses to bind and carry off hearts, as we might use ropes to take
bodies captive.

Such inward recollection of soul, however, is caused not only by an
awareness of God's sacramental presence deep down in the heart, but by
anything at all which makes us aware of his presence. Sometimes all the
powers of our souls are concentrated and withdrawn as a result of the deep
reverence, the undisturbing fear, that takes hold of us as we reflect on the
majesty of the king in whose presence we are, who is looking at us; just
as we should pull ourselves together and collect our thoughts, however

distracted we were, if pope or prince came on the scene, in order to behave with proper respect. We are told that the iris (or gladiolus, as it is sometimes called) closes up its flowers when the sun comes out; it opens them again when the sun goes in, and so they remain open all night. This is what happens in the type of recollection of which I am speaking. The mere presence of God, the mere impression we have that he is looking at us from outside, so to speak, from heaven or anywhere else (even though, for the time being, we have forgotten his presence within us), causes our faculties and powers to concentrate, to recollect themselves, out of reverence for his divine majesty. Love makes us fear him, but it is a fear born of honor, of respect.

I knew a soul,[1] as a matter of fact, to whom you had only to say something (in confession or in private conversation) which reminded her of God's presence a little more vividly than usual, and she would go into such a deep state of recollection that she was hard put to it to emerge from it, to speak and answer you. So much so, that she gave the impression of being lifeless, all her senses deadened, until (sooner or later) the bride-groom allowed her to recover.

(*Treatise* VI, 7)

When the soul is inwardly recollected like that, in God or in his presence, it occasionally becomes so secretly attentive to its beloved's goodness, as to give the appearance of scarcely being attentive at all—so artless its attention, so unobtrusive. Calm, smoothly flowing rivers give a similar impression to those who watch them or sail upon them: there is never a sign of sensation or movement, so even their surface, undisturbed by the merest ripple. It is this delightful stillness of soul that the saintly virgin Teresa of Jesus[2] calls "the prayer of quiet." This is much the same (if I understand her correctly) as the state in which she describes the faculties of the soul as "sleeping."

Even in a human love affair, after all, a man is often content merely to be near, or in sight of his sweetheart. He does not talk to her, he does not even really think about her, or her qualities; he is gratified, it seems, quite

1. Mother Anne-Marie Rosset—an early Visitation nun, also mentioned by Bossuet in his book on prayer.
2. Teresa of Avila, *Way of Perfection,* chapter 32.

content to enjoy her beloved presence, not by reflecting on it, but simply by resting his mind in the peace and quiet it affords.

So completely peaceful does this stillness sometimes become, the soul with all its powers seems to have been lulled to sleep. There is no movement, no activity whatever, except in the will; yet even the will does no more than accept the gratification, the contentment, which the beloved's presence affords. Stranger still, the will is unaware of the gratification and contentment it takes, enjoying it unconsciously; it has no thought for itself, you see, but only for him whose presence affords it delight. A similar sort of thing often happens if we begin to doze in company; we can hear voices but do not take in what is being said, or we can feel a pat on the back and not be conscious of receiving it.

So, if ever you experience this simple, pure, childlike trust in our Lord's presence, dear Theotimus, stay there. Do not try to make any conscious acts, whether of intellect or will. That simple trustful love, that loving spiritual slumber in the Savior's arms, contains to a superlative degree all the things you care for, all the things you go in search of here, there and everywhere. Better to sleep in the sacred heart than to be wakeful anywhere else!

(*Treatise* VI, 8)

A soul that knows stillness and tranquility in God's presence is like a baby at its mother's breast. As that tiny creature satisfies its hunger, its little eyes begin to close, and gradually it falls asleep. All the while, almost imperceptibly, it is still feeding—an unconscious but soothing act. Let the mother deprive it of the breast before it is quite off to sleep—it will waken and cry its heart out, anguish and privation clearly pointing to extreme sweetness of possession.

So it is with the soul. It enjoys, almost without being aware of it, the sweetness of God's presence. It is not busy with its thoughts; only one of its faculties is in use, the very apex of the will, clinging—like the baby at its mother's breast—to the divine presence from which it draws unconscious gratification. Disturb the soul, since it appears to be asleep, try to take away its treasure—it will leave you in no doubt that, though it may be asleep to all things else, it is awake to God. Conscious of the pain of separation, it is upset about it, thus showing the delight it took—however unconsciously—in the good which it possessed. Mother Teresa, in her writings,[1] mentions that she found this analogy a good one; that is why I have thought fit to use it.

What is there, Theotimus, can you tell me, to disquiet a soul recollected in God? Surely it has every reason for being still, and at peace. What is lacking? It has found the one it was looking for, so that all there is left for it to say is: *I have found him, so tenderly loved; and now that he is mine I will never leave him, never let him go* (Sg 3:4). It has no further need of intellectual reasoning; that would be a waste of time, such perfect awareness it has of the bridegroom's presence. Even if he were not visible to the mind, the soul would be quite unconcerned about it, content to sense his presence in the enjoyment, the gratification, which the will gains from it. Think of God's mother, our Lady, our Mistress, during her pregnancy: she could not see her child; but, as she felt him in her womb, only God knows the contentment that was hers! St. Elizabeth too, on the day of the visitation, enjoyed the effects of her Savior's presence in a wonderful way, though she did not see him. Neither has the soul, in its stillness, any further need of memory; it enjoys its lover's presence. No need, either, of imagination; no representation, internal or external, is required of one whose presence is so clearly felt. So that, after all, it is only the will which feeds on that gentle presence; all the other faculties remain in a state of tranquility, charmed by the will's delight.

(Treatise VI, 9)

How to Preserve this Prayer of Quiet or Tranquility

Some people possess active minds, minds that are prolific, swarming with ideas. Others have minds that are flexible, introspective, minds that are greatly given to consciousness of their own working; they must sift all their mental processes; they must be constantly watching themselves to see how they are getting on. There are yet others who are not content with a contented mind, unless they notice, examine and enjoy its content-

---

1. Teresa of Avila, *Way of Perfection,* chapter 32.

ment; they are like people who will not believe themselves to be protected from the cold until they know exactly how many garments they are wearing, who will not admit to being wealthy until they know the exact number of coins in their overfilled coffers.

Usually, people with such types of minds are easy prey to disturbances at prayer. If God affords them the stillness of his presence, they deliberately renounce it by studying their own reactions, by scrutinizing their contentment to see if it is sufficient, anxious to discover whether their peace is really peaceful, their tranquility really tranquil. So much so that, instead of calmly letting their wills experience the charms of God's presence, they busy their minds with analyzing the sensations they experience; like the bride who is so busy looking at the wedding-ring on her finger that she never sees the bridegroom at her side. There is all the difference in the world, Theotimus, between being preoccupied with God who affords us contentment and being completely taken up with the contentment God affords.

Consequently, persons to whom God grants this loving tranquility of soul in prayer must do all they can to refrain from examining either themselves or the stillness they enjoy. If we are to preserve that blissful rest, we must not peer into it inquisitively. The person who is too fond of it loses it; the surest principle for loving it properly is not to become attached to it. Just as a baby will turn from its mother's embrace to see where its feet are, but then come back at once to being cuddled; so, as soon as we are aware of being distracted in prayer by wanting to know what we are doing, we must straightaway bring ourselves back to the gentle placid attentiveness to God's presence from which we turned aside.

Still, it must not be thought that there is any danger of losing this blessed peace through physical or mental activity in which thoughtlessness or carelessness play no part. It would be mere superstition, as the saintly Mother Teresa says,[1] to be so jealous of this stillness as to try not to cough, or sneeze, or even breathe, for fear of losing it. God, who gives this peace, does not take it back on account of essential activity, involuntary distractions or wool-gathering on our part. Once the will has been captivated by God's presence, it never gives up enjoying the happiness of it, even though intellect or memory turns deserter, stealing away in pursuit of irrelevant worthless thoughts.

Obviously, on such occasions, tranquility of soul is not so deep as when

---

1. Teresa of Avila, *Way of Perfection,* chapter 31.

intellect and memory act in concert with the will. For all that, it is still a genuine spiritual peace; its influence pervades the will, and the will has control of all the other faculties.

(Treatise VI, 10)

It follows, from what I have been saying, that there are various degrees of holy tranquility. Sometimes it pervades all the soul's faculties—when they combine to work as one with the will. Sometimes it reigns in the will alone—evident on some occasions, indiscernible on others; now and then, you see, the soul experiences the matchless contentment of actual consciousness, through some form of inward enchantment, that God is present—as happened to St. Elizabeth when our Lady visited her. At other times the soul feels a thrilling charm, as if God were present, though it is not conscious of his presence, as happened to the pilgrim disciples, who were not fully alive to the delightful gratification that stirred them, as they walked along with our Lord, until they reached their destination and *recognized him when he broke bread* (Lk 24:31-35).

Sometimes the soul is not merely conscious of the presence of God, but actually hears him speaking—through those inner lights and convictions that take the place of words. Occasionally, when it hears God's voice, the soul speaks to him so mysteriously, so calmly, so gently, there is no question of losing its blessed peace and tranquility; so still, it would seem to be asleep, yet it is awake to its beloved (cf. Sg 5:2) watching and praying heart to heart with him. At other times the soul hears the bridegroom speak, but cannot talk to him; either reverence, or the sheer joy of listening to him, keeps the soul silent, or else it is experiencing such dryness, such mental inertia, it has no strength for speaking, only for listening. You will occasionally meet with the physical counterpart of spiritual inertia in the case of people who are just dropping off to sleep, or who are greatly enfeebled by some disease.

Finally, however, there are times when the soul neither hears its beloved, nor speaks to him, nor feels any indication of his presence; it simply knows that it is in God's presence, that it is where God wants it to be. Suppose the glorious apostle St. John had fallen into a natural sleep on his dear Lord's breast at the Last Supper, that he had gone to sleep at our Lord's command. Most assuredly, if that were so, he would have been in his master's presence, yet utterly unaware of it.

I would also have you notice that more care is needed to become aware of God's presence than to remain in it once we have that awareness. Hard thinking is demanded, if we are to make the mind attentive to that presence, as I have said in my *Introduction to the Devout Life*.[1] Once in his presence, however, we have several other ways of keeping ourselves there, as long as—using intellect or will—God is the motive and mainspring of what we do. For instance, we can look at him, or something else out of love for him; we can listen to him, or to those who speak in his name; we can talk to him, or to someone else for love of him; we can perform some action, anything at all, to give him glory, to do our duty. In these ways we keep ourselves in God's presence; and not only by listening to him, looking at him, speaking to him, but also by waiting for him to deign to look at us, speak to us, let us talk to him; or even by doing none of these things, but just staying where it suits him to have us, because it suits him to have us there. And if, to this simple process of resting in his presence, he deigns to add the merest consciousness that we are completely his, that he is utterly ours—there is a grace worth having, heaven knows!

Let us go so far, dear Theotimus, as to form another picture for ourselves. Suppose a statue, installed by some sculptor in a palace gallery, were gifted with intelligence, could reason and speak; and suppose you were to ask it: "Tell me, beautiful statue, why are you in that alcove?"

"Why," it would reply, "my master has set me here."

Were you to retort: "But why are you standing there idle?" it would say:

"My master didn't put me here to do anything; he meant me to be motionless."

And if you pressed it further: "But, my dear statue, what is the good of that?"

"Heavens above!" it would answer; "I am not here for my own sake, to do anything for myself; all I'm for is to obey and fulfil my master's, my maker's will—and that's all I want."

"Now look here, statue," suppose you insisted, "perhaps you will tell me, then, how you get any pleasure out of pleasing someone you cannot see?"

"No, indeed, I can't see him," it would admit; "my eyes are not meant for seeing, any more than my feet are meant for walking. Still, I'm quite happy to know that my master sees me here, that he enjoys the sight."

---

1. Part II, chapter 2.

If you were to keep up the argument, and exclaim: "But wouldn't you much prefer to be able to move, to come to the side of the craftsman who made you, so as to be more useful to him?" Undoubtedly it would disagree with you, would insist that it only wanted to do its master's will. "Do you mean to say, then," would be your parting shot, "that all you want to be is a motionless statue in the empty alcove?"

"Exactly!" would come the reply of this wise statue, having the last word; "a statue in this alcove is all I ever want to be, and for as long as my sculptor pleases. I am quite content to be here like this, since it contents the person I belong to, the person who made me what I am."

A good way of staying in his presence, God knows, is if we are, and ever wish to be, entirely at his disposal! Then, I think, whatever we are about—even if we are merely sound asleep—we penetrate still more deeply into the holiness of God's presence. No doubt of that: for, if we are in love with him, our sleep meets with his approval as well as his gaze; we are doing what he wants as well as what he permits. He puts us to bed himself, it seems, that heavenly sculptor, our Creator—as though setting statues in their alcoves—for us to nestle there like birds in their nests. Then, at our waking, if we seriously reflect on it, we discover that God's presence has been enfolding us all the while, that we were never far from him, never cut off from him in the slightest. There we were, in his permissive presence, yet completely unaware of him; so that we could well echo Jacob's words: "Why, I have been sleeping close to my God, cradled in the arms of his presence, his providence; and I was unaware of it (cf. Gn 28:16)!"

But the state of tranquility where the will's sole activity is simply a consent to God's permissive will—content at prayer merely to be in God's sight, if he cares to look—is the best tranquility of all. It is free from all self-seeking. The soul's faculties find no satisfaction there—not even the will, except in its highest point, where it is content to be contented with having no contentment out of love for the contentment of God's permissive will in which it rests. The peak of love's ecstasy, after all, is to long for God's contentment, not our own; is to gratify, not our wishes, but God's.

(*Treatise* VI, 11)

How Love Unites the Soul with God in Prayer

Here, I am not going to discuss habitual union of soul with God, but those special actions, impulses which are the prayers of a recollected soul—its efforts to become more and more united or joined to God's goodness.

Most assuredly, uniting or joining one thing to another is not the same as squeezing one thing against or pressing it upon another. All you need for joining or uniting things is to place them side by side, so that they are touching or together—in the same way as we join vines to elms, or jasmine to the lattice-work of arbors people build in their gardens. For squeezing or pressing, you need to bring a lot more force to bear; this improves and increases union—so that squeezing is an intense, intimate form of joining. You can see this from the way ivy clings to trees. It is not only united to the trees, but pressed or squeezed against them so tightly that it even pierces and penetrates the bark.

We have no call to drop the analogy of a babe's love for its mother; there is such an atmosphere of innocence and purity about it. So picture, then, if you will, a nursing mother sitting down to suckle her child. The sweet little babe eagerly lets itself be gathered into her outstretched arms, curling itself up to be cuddled at her breast. The mother clasps it—glues it, so to speak—to her bosom, kisses it. Her little darling, won by her caresses, concurs in this union. It clings to her, presses as hard as it can against her breast, against her face, as though it meant to bury, to hide itself in the one who gave it birth. There, Theotimus, you have perfect union—a state to which mother and child each contribute. The mother is the cause of it, of course, since she picked the child up, clasped it in her arms, pressed it to her breast; the babe lacks strength enough to squeeze itself so tightly to its mother. For all that, however, the little one does what it can, tries hard to join itself to her. It not merely consents to the union its mother achieves, but wholeheartedly adds its own tiny efforts. If I use the expression "tiny efforts," it is because they are so weak that they seem to be attempts at union on the baby's part, rather than union itself.

Our Savior, in the same way, shows the love of his divine heart to a devoted soul. He attracts the soul, picks it up and, as it were, enfolds all its powers in the bosom of his loving-kindness, which is greater than any mother's could ever be. Burning with love, he clasps the soul, joins it to himself, holds it tight, close to the lips of his delicate charms, locked in his delightful embrace—*A kiss from those lips! Wine cannot ravish the senses like that embrace* (Sg 1:1). The soul, captivated by the delights of these favors, not only assents, not only yields to the union God affords; with all its might it acts in concert, striving to join itself with and cling ever closer to the divine goodness. All the same, the soul is well aware that union—the bond between itself and that supreme loving-kindness—is entirely God's doing; that without his intervention it would be unable to make even the faintest attempts at union.

When people gaze with deep emotion at some exquisite scene, or listen with rapt attention to a beautiful melody, or hang eagerly on every syllable of an exceptional speaker—the eyes of the spectators are said to be glued to the scene, the ears of the audience captivated by the music, their hearts stirred by the speech. What do these expressions mean, except that the senses and faculties referred to are united with, intimately joined to, their several objects? The human soul, to be sure, cleaves to or presses against its object, when it has an intense liking for it; such cleaving, after all, is simply the improvement or intensification of union, of connection. We often use exactly the same expression when we refer to certain moral issues: "he pressed me to do this or that"; "he pressed me to stay." In other words, he not only used persuasion or entreaty, but he used it eagerly, earnestly—like the pilgrims at Emmaus (cf. Lk 24:29), who not only asked our Lord, but pressed him strongly, compelling him with loving violence, to go in and stay with them.

Union with God in prayer is often achieved by tiny but frequent transports or movements of the soul toward God. A child at its mother's breast will often snuggle closer with little pleasurable impulses. In prayer too the heart that is at one with God must be constantly re-charged, to preserve that union, by impulses which clasp it ever closer to God's loving-kindness. For instance, if a soul has experienced a fairly lengthy state of conscious union, in which it has relished the intense happiness of belonging to God, it ultimately increases union by uplifting the heart in a transport of love: "Yes, Lord, I am yours, absolutely, entirely, utterly, without reserve." Or perhaps: "Yours I am, Lord, that is certain; and I want to be so ever more and more." Or even, by way of petition: "Sweet Jesus, draw me ever deeper into your heart, where your love may swallow me up, where I may be utterly lost in its enchantment."

At other times, however, union is not achieved by repeated impulses, but by a continuous unconscious stirring or movement of the heart toward God. A huge heavy mass of lead, bronze or stone, free from all external pressure, pushes, sinks and buries itself in the ground by reason of its weight and the pull of gravity. The human heart too, once it is joined to God, sinks ever deeper into union with him as long as it is not turned aside. Charity makes it tend ever closer to the supreme goodness by an imperceptible growth in union until the heart is wholly at rest in God. "Love," as the apostle of France says,[1] "is a unitive virtue"; in other words, a virtue that makes us perfectly at one with God, our supreme good. Unquestionably charity is something active in this life, or at least it is a habit that leads to activity; so that, even when it has achieved perfect union, it still remains active—however imperceptibly—in order to deepen and cement that union still further.

Blessed, indeed, are those who lovingly preserve the awareness of God's presence in the stillness of their hearts; they will be drawing ever closer to God—imperceptible though it may seem—their whole soul filled with the infinite charm of it. By the awareness of God's presence, in this context, I do not mean a sense awareness, but one which has its place in the apex, the highest point of the soul, where the love of God is supreme, where it is chiefly practiced.

(*Treatise* VII, 1)

Occasionally union is achieved without any corresponding effort on our part; we merely go along unresistingly, allowing God, in his goodness, to unite us with him. This is what a baby does: it longs to be nursed by its mother, but is too weak to lift itself up to her embrace, or cling to her once she is holding it; it is only too happy to be picked up, cradled in its mother's arms, clasped to her breast.

Sometimes, when God attracts us, we actually lend our own efforts. We do this if, when he draws us (cf. Sg 1:3), we hasten eagerly to act in concert with the gentle strength of his goodness as it allures us, clasps us to his embrace in love.

Sometimes we appear to begin to unite ourselves closely with God before he joins himself to us; that is because we are conscious of what *we* are doing to achieve union, but unaware of God's part in the process. No question, however, but that it is always due to his prompting, even though

1. St. Denis, *The Divine Names,* 4.

we are not always conscious of his inspirations. Never should we become one with God unless he first united himself with us. He anticipates our choice and possession of him by his choice and possession of us. Once let us follow his imperceptible attraction, once let us begin to unite ourselves to him . . . then he frequently furthers our attempts at union, coming to the aid of our weakness, giving us an awareness of his closeness so that we actually feel him making his way into our hearts—an experience, in its enchantment, beyond compare.

Sometimes too, after attracting us to union without our being aware of it, he continues to help us, continues to promote union, while we remain unconscious of his efforts. We have no idea how such close union results; we know only that it is beyond our own unaided strength. This leads us to conclude that some mysterious power is secretly at work in us. We are like captains of sailing ships laden with cargoes of iron. As soon as they feel their craft beginning to scud along when the wind has dropped, they know that they are near hills whose magnetic force is secretly pulling them in that direction; in this way they note a recognizable, detectable progress caused by unrecognized, undetected contours. In exactly the same way, when we experience an ever closer union of our souls with God in spite of only tiny efforts on the will's part, we come to the conclusion—since we have insufficient wind for such progress—that the lover of our souls is attracting us by the invisible influence of his grace. He means that influence to be imperceptible, for us to find it more wonderful; he wants us to be unconcerned about feeling his attractions, to busy ourselves purely and simply with being united to his divine goodness.

Sometimes union is so insensible that we neither feel God at work in us, nor our co-operation. In fact we find union achieved without noticing it; like Jacob, who found himself matched unawares with Lia; or rather, like Samson (only in happier circumstances), we find ourselves seemingly caught and bound by union, without our having been aware of it. At other times we are aware of the binding process taking place by activity—on God's part and ours—of which we are conscious.

Sometimes union is achieved in and by means of the will alone. Occasionally too the intellect plays its part; the will draws it after it, directing its attention to what the will is engrossed in, affording it a special pleasure in its concentration. After all, we often find love concentrating the gaze of our eyes, fixing them on what we love.

Sometimes the union is achieved by all the soul's faculties gathering round the will, not to unite themselves to God—they are quite incapable of that—but to make it easier for the will to achieve union. If those other faculties were each engrossed in their own functions, the soul would be unable to undertake as perfectly the activity by which union with God is achieved.

Such are the various kinds of union.

With us, Christ's love is a compelling motive (2 Cor 5:14). A wonderful example of perfect union he offers us, heaven knows! He united himself with our human nature from the first, engrafting it on to his, so that to some extent it might share his life. When Adam's sin ruptured that union, God provided a closer, stronger union in the incarnation, in which our human nature found itself for ever wedded to the personality of the Godhead. Then, so that all people individually might be intimately united to his goodness—not merely human nature as such—he instituted the sacrament of the holy eucharist, which each can share and so achieve personal union with the Savior, in reality and by way of food. It is this sacramental union, Theotimus, which impels us toward and promotes that union of soul with God I am now discussing.

(*Treatise* VII, 2)

The Highest Degree of Union: Ecstasy or Rapture

In whatever way union of soul with God is achieved, then—consciously or unconsciously—God is always responsible for it. No one can become one with God without going out toward him; nor can anyone go out toward God unless attracted by him. The divine bridegroom made this clear, when he said: *Nobody can come to me without being attracted toward me by the Father who sent me* (Jn 6:44). The bride in the Song of Songs also expressed the same idea in her exclamation: *Draw me after thee where thou wilt; see, we hasten after thee, by the very fragrance of those perfumes allured* (Sg 1:3)!

Two things are needed for this union to be perfect: it must be unadulterated, it must be strong. After all, I can go up to people to talk to them perhaps, or to see them better, or collect something from them, or enjoy the perfume they are wearing, or lean on them. Undoubtedly, at such times, I approach them, attach myself to them; but the approach, the union, are not my main ambition—I am only using them as ways and means for getting something else. However, if I go to someone, attach myself to him or her for no other reason than to be near this person, to enjoy that proximity, that union—then the approach I make is for union pure and simple.

People approach our Lord in similar ways. Some come to listen to him, like Mary Magdalen; others to be cured, like the woman who had an issue of blood; others to adore him, like the wise men; others to serve him, like Martha; others to overcome their disbelief, like St. Thomas; others to embalm him, like Magdalen, Joseph, Nicodemus. The Sulamite in the Song of Songs, however, searches for him in order to find him, and only wants to find him in order to hold him close, never to let go of him: *I found him,* she said; *and now that he is mine I will never leave him, never let him go* (Sg 3:4). Jacob (as St. Bernard remarks), when he held God in a firm grip, was willing to let him go as long as he received a blessing (Gn 32:26); but the Sulamite will not let him go for all the blessings he has to give. It was not God's blessings she wanted, but God himself from whom all blessings come. An echo of David's cry: *What else does heaven hold for me but thyself? What charm for me has earth, here at thy side? What though flesh of mine, heart of mine, should waste away? Still God will be my heart's stronghold, eternally my inheritance* (Ps 72:25, 26). So it was with our Lord's glorious Mother beside the cross.

"What are you seeking, Mother of life," they might have asked her, "on that hill of Calvary, that place or death?"

"My Son," she would have answered, "my life's life, that is whom I am seeking."

"But why are you looking for him?"

"So as to be near him."

"But death's noose is about him now; the grave has caught him in its toils" (cf. Ps 17:5; 114:3).

"Oh, but it is not happiness that I am looking for; he himself is all I seek. The love of my heart has me seeking everywhere for the child of my love, my dearly loved Son."

What it comes to, you see, is this: such union breeds in the soul one only aim—to be with its beloved.

However, when union between the soul and God is exceptionally close and intimate, it is called inhesion, or adhesion, by the theologians. The reason is that such union holds the soul captive, clinging, pressed and fastened to his divine majesty in such a way that it can scarcely disengage or free itself. Look, for a moment, at that man over there—his attention caught and held by the charm of some haunting melody, or (to turn from the sublime to the ridiculous) by a trifling game of cards. Try to get him away; you cannot. No matter what demands his attention at home, he will not be torn away, even food and drink forgotten. What, then, of the soul in love with God? Heaven knows, it should find itself held in a much stronger grip—united as it is to the infinite loving-kindness of God—when it finds itself captive, enamored of perfections beyond compare! So it was with that chosen instrument of God (Acts 9:15), who exclaimed: *With Christ* I am fastened to *the cross, so that I may live to God* (Gal 2:19). He was persuaded too that nothing, not even death, would separate him from his master (Rom 8:38, 39).

Now, as the saintly Mother Teresa says so well,[1] when union has reached such perfection as to hold us captive, clinging to our Savior, it is identical with rapture, suspension of the faculties, elevation of soul. Only, it is called union, or suspension, or elevation, when it is of short duration; but ecstasy, or rapture, when it lasts for a long time. The plain fact is that the soul is so closely, so tightly bound to God, it cannot easily be separated from him; actually it has gone out of itself into God. It is as much a part of him as a crucified body is part of the cross to which it is fastened, or ivy is part of the wall to which it clings.

To avoid any ambiguity, however, I would have you know that it is charity which binds us, that charity *is the bond which makes us perfect* (Col 3:14); and the more charity a person has, the closer is his union and intimacy with God. Now I am not referring here to that habitual state of union we may experience sleeping or waking; I am speaking of active union which comes from love and charity in action.

Pretend that St. Paul, St. Denis, St. Augustine, St. Bernard, St. Francis of Assisi, St. Catherine of Genoa are alive today; that they are sleeping, worn out by all the work they have done out of love for God. At the same time picture some good soul—not so saintly, however—enjoying the prayer of union. Tell me, Theotimus, who is more united, closer to, more captivated by God—those great saints in their sleep, or that person at prayer? The saints, of course; you can be sure of that. Their charity is greater; their affections, though to some extent dormant, are so concen-

---

1. Teresa of Avila, *Life,* chapters 18, 20.

trated, so caught up in their master, it is impossible to tear them away from him. But if it puzzles you how anyone in the prayer of union, in ecstasy almost, is not so closely united to God as those who are asleep, however saintly they may be, remember this: The individual at prayer experiences a union which is more active, but the sleeping saints know a deeper actual union. The saints already enjoy union; they are not striving after it, since they are asleep. But the soul at prayer is clearly striving after union, being actually engaged in that activity.

This practice of union with God, however, can even be performed by brief, transitory but frequent yearnings of the heart for God. . . . "If only mine were the grace, good Jesus, to be utterly one with you! At last, Lord, putting behind me the manifold variety of created things, all I crave is your unity! My God, you are the *only one thing necessary* (Lk 10:42), the only unity my soul needs! Unite, dear friend of my heart, this unique little soul of mine to your unparalleled goodness. You are all mine, when shall I be all yours? Lord Jesus, my beloved, be the magnet of my heart; clasp, press, unite me for ever to your sacred heart! You have made me for yourself, how is it that I am not one with you? Absorb this tiny drop of life you have given me into the ocean of your goodness whence it came. Since your heart loves me, Lord, why doesn't it take me out of myself to you?—especially as that is all I want! Draw me, and I shall hasten after your allurements (cf. Sg 1:3), to throw myself into your fatherly arms and never stir from that embrace for ever and ever. Amen."

                                                                    (*Treatise* VII, 3)

Types of Ecstasy or Rapture

Ecstasy is given the name of rapture, since it is a state in which God attracts us and lifts us up to him. Rapture is called ecstasy, because it takes us out of ourselves, holds us above and beyond self, to make us one with God. Wonderfully gentle, charming, delightful as God's attractions are, his goodness and beauty exert such a powerful influence on the soul's attention and concentration that it would seem we are not merely uplifted, but transported, swept away. On the other hand, wholehearted assent and fervent impulse speed the soul in the wake of God's attractions, so that it seems as though it not only rises and ascends, but throws itself, soars out of itself into the very Godhead.

When it comes to spiritual ecstasies, they are of three kinds: ecstasy of intellect, ecstasy of will, ecstasy of activity. The first is toward enlightenment, the second toward fervor, the third toward good works; the first is caused by wonderment, the second by devotion, the third by exercise.

Wonderment is the result of our meeting with a new truth that we neither knew nor expected to know. If this new truth also contains beauty and goodness, then the wonderment to which it gives rise is delightful in the extreme. That is why the queen of Sheba, when she found Solomon to be a wiser man than she had ever dreamed, stood breathless in wonder (cf. 1 Kgs 10:5). The Jews too, when they saw that our Lord possessed a wisdom beyond their belief, were overcome with astonishment (cf. Mt 13:54-56). So, when God deigns to endow our minds with a special enlightenment through which they reach unusual heights in the contemplation of his mysteries, then they grow in wonderment as they discern more beauty there than they had ever imagined.

The wonderment aroused in us by things which please us firmly fixes and concentrates the mind on the objects of our wonderment; this follows both from the perfection of the beauty discerned in them and from the unusualness of that perfection. The intellect never tires of examining what it has never known before, what is so pleasing to the mind. In addition to this, God occasionally gives the soul a light that is not only penetrating, but ever growing in brightness like the dawn of a new day. This leads the mind to bury itself deeper and deeper in concentration on wonderment at the God it is coming to know; just as those who strike gold delve still further to unearth more of that coveted metal. Philosophy and science are the result of wonderment; and so, in exactly the same way, are contemplation and mystical theology. Since wonderment, if it is extreme, lifts us out of ourselves by eager attentiveness and concentration of mind upon heavenly things, it cannot but result in ecstasy.

(*Treatise* VII, 4)

God attracts the human mind by his supreme beauty, his inexhaustible goodness—perfections of one supreme Godhead, uniquely good, uniquely beautiful, at one and the same time. What is good or beautiful is the cause of all activity; all things are attracted to it, moved by it, gripped by it, because they love it. What is good, what is beautiful, is also desirable, lovable, dear to everyone; it is the reason for every activity, every choice.

God, in the same way, *the Father of all that gives light* (Jas 1:17), supremely good and beautiful, in his beauty leads our minds to contemplate him, in his goodness leads our wills to love him. His beauty, delighting our minds, brings to birth in our wills a love for him; his goodness, filling our wills with love for him, stimulates our minds to contemplate him—love prompting contemplation, contemplation prompting love.

Ecstasy and rapture, therefore, are results of love; love is what leads the mind to contemplation, the will to union. So that, in the end, we must come to St. Denis' conclusion that "divine love is ecstatic—lovers may not be alive to themselves, but only to the God they love." This is why that wonderful apostle, St. Paul, full of love for God, feeling its ecstatic influence, was inspired to say: *I am alive; or rather, not I; it is Christ that lives in me* (Gal 2:20). Lifted out of himself to God, like a true lover, his life was no longer his own, but his beloved's, who is to be loved above all things.

Love's rapture seizes upon the will in this way: God touches it with the charms of his loving-kindness; then, just as a compass-needle, forgetting it cannot feel, turns toward the pole, so the will, stricken with love for heavenly things, soars up, reaches out toward God, turning its back on all earthly attachments. In this way it begins to experience a rapture, not of wonderment but of fervor, not of perception but of experience, not of sight but of taste, of relish. Indeed, as I have already pointed out, the mind sometimes begins to wonder at the delight which the will experiences during an ecstasy; just as the will often thrills with pleasure when it perceives that the mind is lost in wonderment. So that these two faculties transmit their raptures each to the other: the contemplation of beauty leads us to love it, the love of beauty leads us to contemplate it. Rarely does the sun warm people without shining on them, nor shine upon them without warming them; so love leads easily to wonderment, while wonderment leads naturally to love.

For all that, these two ecstasies of intellect and will are not so essentially inseparable that one cannot often exist without the other. Just as philosophers have had greater knowledge of the Creator than love for him, so good Christians have many a time had more love than knowledge. Consequently, exceptional knowledge is not always followed by tremendous love, any more than a tremendous love is always followed by exceptional knowledge—as I have said before.[1] If the ecstasy of wonder-

---

1. Book VI, chapter 4.

ment is all that we experience, we are none the better for it—according to that man who *was carried up into the third heaven* (2 Cor 12:2): *No secret hidden from me, no knowledge too deep for me,* he said; *yet if I lack charity, I count for nothing* (1 Cor 13:2).

(Treatise VII, 5)

To help us distinguish divine ecstasies from human or diabolical ones, God's servants have left considerable evidence. For my own part, it will sufficiently meet my purpose here if I give you two signs of sound and saintly ecstasy. The first is that a holy ecstasy never takes over, engages the intellect to the extent that it does the will, which it moves, excites, fills with a powerful fondness for God. So that if an ecstasy is more beautiful than good, more discerning than fervent, more speculative than stimulating, it is extremely dubious, highly suspect. I do not mean that raptures, visions (even of a prophetic type), are impossible without charity (cf. 1 Cor 13:2); I am well aware that, as we can have charity and yet not be enraptured or prophesy, so we can experience raptures, have powers of prophecy, and yet not have charity. What I do mean, however, is that when persons have more light in their intellect to appreciate God's wonders than fervor in their will to love God, then they must be on their guard: there is every likelihood that their ecstasy may be a fake, may elate rather than edify—classing them, indeed, like Saul (cf. 1 Sm 10:11, 12), Balaam (cf. Nm 22), Caiphas (cf. Jn 11:51), among the prophets, yet leaving them all the time among the damned.

The second sign of an authentic ecstasy lies in the third kind of ecstasy which I mentioned above[1]—an ecstasy that is perfectly holy, perfectly desirable, crowning the other two; this is the ecstasy of activity, of life. Absolute observance of God's commandments is beyond the bounds of human strength; however, it is still well within the compass of the natural instincts of the human heart—eminently consistent with the natural light of reason. In other words, if we live our lives in accordance with God's commandments, we are doing nothing foreign to our natural tendency. However, besides God's commandments there are inspirations of grace. If we are to fulfil these, God has not only to uplift us beyond our own strength, but also to pull us above the instincts, the tendencies of our

---

1. Book VII, chapter 4.

nature. For although inspirations are not opposed to human reason, yet they do transcend it; they outstrip it, take precedence over it. So that at such times it is not merely a normal decent Christian life that we are living, but one that is superhuman, spiritual, devoted, ecstatic; in other words, a life that is in every way beyond and above our natural state.

Never to steal, or tell lies, never to be impure, or swear unnecessarily, or take another's life; ever to say one's prayers, love and respect one's parents—all that amounts to living in accord with human natural reason. But to give up all our possessions, to love poverty, to call it "lady" and mean it, to count disgrace, scorn, abasement, persecution, martyrdom as blessings, as sources of intense happiness, to accept the limitations of absolute chastity, to behave (after all) in complete contrast to the opinions and maxims of the world in which we live, to swim against the stream by habitual self-renouncement and submission—there is life, not on the natural, but on the supernatural level; that is living, not within, but above and beyond ourselves. Since nobody can go out of self in this way, unless to be attracted by the eternal Father (Jn 6:44), such a way of living necessitates a continual rapture, a permanent ecstasy of activity and work.

You have undergone death, wrote St. Paul to the people of Rhodes,[1] *and your life is hidden away now with Christ in God* (Col 3:3). Death sets the soul free from the limitations of the body; so what does the apostle mean by his statement, *You have undergone death?* It is as though he had said: "You are alive to self no longer, free from the limitations of your natural state; your soul's life is no longer its own, but God's." It is the nature of the phoenix to destroy its own life under the scorching sun—hiding it, so to speak, beneath the ashes—to rise to a finer, stronger life. Silk-worms change into butterflies. Bees are born as little worms, then they become crawling nymphs, and finally flying insects. So it is with us, Theotimus, if we are spiritual. We lay aside our natural life, to lead a higher one, hiding this new life completely *with Christ in God,* who alone sees it, understands it, bestows it.

This new life of ours is charity, enlivening and quickening the soul; this love is quite hidden away with Christ in God, in the things of God. In heaven, in God, Jesus Christ is hidden away, since (as the sacred text of the gospel informs us [cf. Mk 16:19; Lk 24:51; Acts 1:9]) though the disciples saw him lifted up at his ascension, very soon *a cloud caught him*

---

1. According to some Greek writers the Colossians lived at Rhodes, and were so called after the famous Colossus.

away from their sight. Now, Jesus Christ is our love; and our love is the life of our souls. *Our life, then, is hidden away with Christ* (who is our love) *in God;* so that when Christ, the life of the spirit, *is made manifest* on the day of judgment, we *too will be made manifest in glory with him* (Col 3:4)—in other words, Jesus Christ, our love, will give glory to us, sharing with us his bliss, his splendor.

(Treatise VII, 6)

How Love is the Life of the Soul

The soul is the active principle of all humanity's vital impulses; it is, in Aristotle's words, "the principle of life, sensation, intelligence." Different kinds of life, in consequence, are recognized by different kinds of movement; this means that any animal which has no natural movement is completely lifeless. Love, in the same way, is the active principle of the spiritual life, the life of devotion; it gives us vitality, sensitivity, emotion. Our spiritual lives are what love's activity makes them: a heart devoid of emotion is devoid of love; while a loving heart cannot be devoid of love's emotion. So that as soon as we have given our love to Jesus Christ, we have—by the fact itself—given into his keeping our spiritual life. At present, however, he is hidden away with God in heaven, just as the divinity was hidden in him during his earthly life. That is why our life is hidden away now in him; but when he is made manifest in glory, our life and our love will also be made manifest with him in God.

So St. Ignatius of Antioch (as St. Denis tells us) used to say that his love was crucified. It was as though he were saying: "My natural human love, with all its passions, is fastened by the cross. I have put it to death for the mortal love it is; the life it gave my heart was only mortal. As my Savior was crucified, as he died to his mortal life in order to rise to one that is immortal, I have died with him on the cross to my natural love, my soul's mortal life, so as to rise to the supernatural life of a love that—active as it will be in heaven—is consequently immortal too."

Therefore, if we see someone experiencing raptures in prayer, being carried out of self into God, and yet experiencing no ecstasy of life—in other words, failing to live a life that is self-sacrificing, devoted to God, by renouncing all worldly lusts, by mortifying all desires, all natural tendencies, by an inward meekness, simplicity, humility, but most of all by unceasing charity—depend upon it, Theotimus, all those raptures are extremely dubious, fraught with danger. Raptures of that kind pander to human wonderment, but do not make for holiness. What is the good of being rapt in God at prayer, if our lives, our activities, are rapt in the love of earthly, shallow, natural things? To be lifted above self in prayer, but to fall below self in life, in activity; to be angelic in meditation, but beastly in company—what is that but *to waver between two loyalties, to take oaths to the Lord* (1 Kgs 18:21) and *swear by Milcom* (Zep 1:5)? It is a genuine sign, after all, that such raptures, such ecstasies are nothing but deceptions and delusions of the evil one.

Blessed are those who live a supernatural ecstatic life, surpassing themselves, yet have never been rapt above themselves in prayer! There are many souls in heaven who never had an ecstasy, never experienced a rapture in contemplation. History is full of martyrs, of very saintly people of both sexes, whose only privilege in prayer was to experience devotion and fervor. However, there has never been a saint who did not know the ecstasy, the rapture of life, of activity, by rising above self and its natural tendencies.

It should be quite clear to everybody, you will agree, that this ecstasy of life and activity was in the forefront of St. Paul's mind, when he wrote: *I am alive; or rather, not I; it is Christ that lives in me* (Gal 2:20). He gives the explanation himself, in different words, to the Romans. *Our former nature has been crucified with him,* he tells them; *we have died with Christ* to sin; we have also risen with him, that *we too might live and move in a new kind of existence, so that we are the slaves of guilt no longer* (Rom 6:4-11). This means that each one of us typifies two people; and, consequently, appears to have two lives. One of them is *the old self* (Col 3:9, 10), our old life—when we are like aging eagles, dragging our wings, unable to fly; the other is *the new self,* our new life—when we are like eagles that have cast off useless feathers and, with plumage restored, recapture their youth, taking wing on new-found strength (cf. Ps 102:5).

In the first of these lives we live by the pattern of *the old self*—in other words, the defects, the want of character, the failings that we inherit from the sin of our first parent; consequently, we are living under the shadow of Adam's sin, and our life is a mortal life, or rather a living death. In the second of these lives we live by the pattern of *the new self*—in other words, the graces, blessings, providence and will of our Savior; as a result, we are living in the light of salvation, of redemption, and this new life is a spirited, energetic, invigorating one.

However, those who mean to rise to the new life must do so by dint of dying to the old one, crucifying *nature, with all its passions, all its impulses* (Gal 5:24), burying it in the waters of baptism or of penance. They must imitate Naaman (cf. 2 Kgs 5:14), who drowned his former life, tainted with leprosy, in the waters of Jordan in order to enjoy a new life that was clean and healthy. Naaman, it could be said, was never his old self again.

Anyone, therefore, who is raised up to the Savior's new life, no longer lives by, in, or for self; rather, he or she is living with, in, and for the Savior. *And you, too,* says St. Paul, *must think of yourselves as dead to sin, and alive with a life that looks toward God, through Christ Jesus our Lord* (Rom 6:11).

(Treatise VII, 7)

More Letters on Prayer

To Madame de Granieu

Your kind of prayer is very good, indeed much better than if you made many reflections and used many words, for these are only meant to arouse our affections; if God is pleased to give us affections without the reflections and words, this is a great grace. The secret of secrets in prayer is to follow our attraction in simplicity of heart. Take the trouble to read, or to have read to you if it is too much for your eyes, the seventh book of the *Treatise on the Love of God;* you will find there all you need to know about prayer.

I remember that one day when you told me in confession how you prayed, I said that it was a very good way and that although you ought to prepare a point for meditation, if God drew you to a particular affection as soon as you came into his presence, then you were not to hold on to the point, but follow the affection; the more simple and peaceful it is, the better, for then it will bind your soul more closely to its object. Once you have resolved to follow your affection, dearest daughter, don't waste time during prayer trying to understand exactly what you are doing or how you are praying; for the best prayer is that which keeps us so occupied with

God that we don't think about ourselves or about what we are doing. In short, we must go to prayer simply, in good faith, and artlessly, wanting to be close to God so as to love him, to unite ourselves to him. True love has scarcely any method.

Be at peace, my dearest daughter, and walk faithfully along the path which God has marked out for you. Take care to bring contentment to him to whom God has espoused you; like a honey bee, while you are carefully making the honey of devotion, at the same time make the wax of your household affairs; for if honey is sweet to the taste of our Lord who ate butter and honey while on earth, wax also honors him since it used to make the candles which give light to those around us.

(*Letters*, p. 167)

To Madame de Chantal

I'd like to say more about your prayer, for I reread your letter late last night. Go on doing as you described. Be careful not to intellectualize, because this can be harmful, not only in general, but especially at prayer. Approach the beloved object of your prayer with your affections quite simply and as gently as you can. Naturally, every now and then, your intellect will make an effort to apply itself; don't waste time trying to guard against this, for that would only be a distraction. When you notice this happening, be content simply to return to acts of the will.

Staying in God's presence and placing ourselves in God's presence are, to my mind, two different things. In order to place ourselves in his presence we have to withdraw our soul from every other object and make it attentive to that presence at this very moment, as I have explained in the book.[1] But once we are there, we remain there, as long as either our intellect or our will is active in regard to God. We look either at him or at something else for love of him; or, not looking at anything at all, we speak to him; or again, without either looking at him or speaking to him, we just stay there where he has placed us, like a statue in its niche. And if while we are there, we also have some sense that we belong to God and that he is our all, then we must certainly thank him for this.

---

1. I.e., *Introduction* II, 2.

Dear daughter, what a good way of praying, and what a fine way of staying in God's presence: doing what he wants and accepting what pleases him! It seems to me that Mary Magdalene was a statue in her niche when, without saying a word, without moving, and perhaps even without looking at him, she sat at our Lord's feet and listened to what he was saying. When he spoke, she listened; whenever he paused, she stopped listening; but always, she was right there (Lk 10:39).[1] A little child who is at its mother's breast when she has fallen asleep is really where it belongs and wants to be, even though neither of them makes a sound.

O my daughter, how I enjoy talking with you about these things! How happy we are when we want to love our Lord! Let's really love him, my daughter, and let's not start examining in detail what we are doing for love of him, as long as we know that we never want to do anything except for love of him. For my part, I think we remain in God's presence even while we are asleep, because we fall asleep in his sight, as he pleases, and according to his will, and he puts us down on our bed like a statue in its niche; when we wake up, we find him still there, close by. He has not moved, nor have we; evidently, we have stayed in his presence, but with our eyes closed in sleep.[2]

(*Letters*, pp. 151-53)

---

1. Cf. *Treatise* VI, 8.
2. Cf. *Treatise* VI, 11.

In Life

The Signified or "Declared" Will of God

Occasionally we think of God's will in itself. We find it utterly holy and good, so that we are ready to praise, bless and adore it, ready to make a sacrifice of our own wills, and of the wills of all other creatures, in obedience to God, our Lord's plea on our lips: *Thy will be done, on earth as it is in heaven* (Mt 6:10). At other times we think of God's will in terms of what it does on any given occasion—circumstances that befall us, events that happen, anything that shows or tells us what God wants. Although God's will is unique and simple, we call it by several names, depending on how we come to know it—a variety of ways which load us with a variety of obligations to comply with it.

Christian doctrine clearly sets forth the truths God wants us to believe, the blessings he means us to hope for, the punishments he intends us to fear, the things he would like us to love, the commandments he means us to keep and the counsels he wishes us to follow. All that goes by the name of God's "declared" will, because he has declared and revealed to us that he means and expects us to believe, hope, fear, love and perform it all.

Since God's declared will is an expression of his desire, not of his positive will, we can either follow it by obedience or oppose it by disobedience. Our ability to refuse to do what he wants has demanded three activities on the part of God's will: he means us to be able to oppose his will, he wants us to refrain from opposing it, yet he allows us to oppose it if we so desire. Our ability to oppose God's will we owe to our natural state, to our freedom; our actual opposition is the result of our ill will; to refrain from opposing him is to comply with his desire. If we oppose his will, therefore, God lends no support to our disobedience; he simply leaves us *to the arbitrament of our own wills* (Sir 15:14) allowing the choice of evil. When we obey him, however, God lends his aid, his inspiration, his grace.

Permission is an act of the will, but a barren, sterile, fruitless act; it is a passive action, you might say, which does nothing, merely lets something happen. Desire, on the contrary, is an activity that is fruitful, fertile; it impels us forward, beckons us, spurs us on. That is why God, when he wants us to follow his declared will, entreats, encourages, impels, inspires, aids and abets us; when he allows us to oppose his will, however, he simply leaves us to our own devices, free to please ourselves, to thwart his plans.

God's desire is genuine, for all that. Suppose you want to give one of your friends a good time: you invite him out to a meal—like the king in our Lord's parable (cf. Mt 22:2-10; Lk 14:16-23); you beg him to come, to sit down to a spread, to enjoy himself. Most assuredly, you do not force open your friend's mouth, stuff the food down his throat, make him swallow it; he is not an animal you are fattening for Christmas. Courtesy and kindness demand that you tempt him, not compel him, with such a favor; so you express it as something you would like him to do, not something you mean him to have at all costs. So it is with God's declared will. He genuinely desires us to do what he makes known to us; for that reason he gives us all we need for the purpose, begs and prays us to use it. More than that he cannot be expected to do. Sunbeams are still genuine rays of light from the sun, even when something impedes their progress. God's declared will, in the same way, is still God's genuine will, even if it is resisted—though it is not so effective as when it is complied with.

We comply with God's declared will, then, whenever we accept what God shows us to be his plans—when we believe what he teaches, trust in his promises, fear his threats, love his commands and counsels, and live by them. What else is the point of those things we do so often in our ceremonies? For instance, we stand for the reading of the gospel as a sign that we are ready to obey God's declared will which it contains; we kiss the book, when the reading is over, in token of our reverence for the word which declares to us the will of heaven. So it was that many of the saints in olden days used to carry a portion of the gospels near their hearts—as we read of St. Cecilia. Indeed, when St. Barnabas died, a copy of St. Matthew's gospel, in Barnabas's own writing, was found next his heart. That was why a large throne was erected amid the assembled bishops during the early councils of the Church: it held the book of the gospels which represented the person of Christ—king, doctor, director, spirit and heart of the Church and of its councils—so great was their reverence for God's will expressed in that book. Indeed, the great model of pastoral life, St. Charles, archbishop of Milan, always studied holy scripture bareheaded, on his knees, to show how respectfully we should hear or read God's declared will.

(*Treatise* VIII, 3)

God has revealed in so many ways, by so many means, that he intends us all to be saved, no human being can be unaware of the fact. That is why at the creation he made us *wearing* his *own image and likeness* (Gn 1:26, 27); why he himself wore our image and likeness at the incarnation, and later suffered death to redeem the whole human race, to save it. Love was his motive to such an extent that—as St. Denis, the apostle of France, relates—he one day told the saintly Carpus that he was "ready to suffer all over again for humanity's salvation," that he would be glad to do this provided it involved no person's sin.

Even though everyone does not win salvation, it is still a genuine will on God's part, whose activity is in accord both with his nature and with ours. His goodness leads him to shower over us his helping graces, so that we may reach the bliss of his glory. However, our nature demands that God's liberality should leave us our liberty—to use his generous graces and be saved, or to remain indifferent to them and be lost.

We must intend our own salvation, Theotimus, in the way God intends it. God desires that we should be saved; we too need constantly to desire what God desires. God not only means us to be saved, but he actually gives us all we need to achieve salvation; so we are not to stop at merely desiring salvation, but go a step further and accept all the graces God has prepared for us, the graces he offers us. It is all very well to say: "I want to be saved." It is not much use merely saying: "I want to take the necessary steps." For that, we need to make a definite resolution to take and use the graces God holds out to us; our wills must be in tune with his. Since God wants us to be saved, we should want to be saved; we should also welcome the means to salvation that God intends us to take.

It often happens, however, that the way to salvation is acceptable in outline, but dreadful in detail. You will remember St. Peter . . . ready to suffer anything, even death, to bear his Master company; yet, when it came to the point, he grew pale, trembled, even denied his Master at the charge of a servant-girl (Lk 22:23, 56, 57). Each one of us thinks he has strength enough to drink the Lord's cup with him (Mt 20:22); but when it is actually offered, we run away, we give it all up. What we foresee in detail makes a stronger impression on the imagination—that is why, in my *Introduction to the Devout Life*,[1] I suggested that general acts of prayer should always be followed by particular resolutions. David was accepting particular trials as a means to perfection when he exclaimed: *It was in*

---

1.   Part II, chapter 6.

mercy thou didst chasten me, Lord, *schooling me to thy obedience* (Ps 118:71). The apostles too rejoiced over their torments, because *they had been found worthy to suffer indignity for the sake of Jesus' name* (Acts 5:41).

(Treatise VIII, 4)

God's Will Declared in the Counsels

A command reveals a definite intention on the part of the person giving the order; a counsel betrays only a desire. A command obliges us; a counsel merely invites. A commandment renders those who break it blameworthy; a counsel simply renders those who fail to follow it less worthy of praise. Those who break the commandments deserve to be damned; those who neglect the counsels simply deserve to enjoy a lower place in glory.

Command and commend are two different things: commanding, a person supplies an obligation by the use of authority; commending, he or she offers an inducement by the use of friendship. A commandment imposes necessity; a counsel, a recommendation, suggests greater utility. The answer to a command is obedience, to a counsel confidence. Our aim is to please, if we follow a counsel; we keep a commandment, so as not to displease. That is why gratifying love, which binds us to please the beloved, naturally leads us to follow his counsels; and why benevolent love, intent on submitting to him every decision and choice, causes us not only to want what he commands, but also what he counsels, what he suggests. A child's love and respect for its father, after all, inspires it to do not only what it is told, but also what it sees the parent would like.

Clearly a counsel is given for the sake of the person it is directed to, as an aid to perfection: *If thou hast a mind to be perfect,* was the Savior's way for expressing it, *go home, and sell all that belongs to thee; give it to the poor . . . then come back and follow me* (Mt 19:21; Lk 18:22). However, the utility of a counsel weighs little with a loving heart; all it aims at is complying with God's wishes, paying him the respect due to his will. So it accepts the counsels in the way God intends; and God does not intend each person to keep all the counsels. He means a person to keep only those counsels which are appropriate to the time, to the occasion, to the individual, to his or her abilities, according as charity demands. It is charity, queen of virtues, queen of all commandments, all counsels, of every Christian law and activity, which gives to each its rank, its order, its occasion and importance.

If your father or mother need you to support them, this is no time to carry out the counsel of retiring to a convent. Charity orders you to set about fulfilling its command of honoring, serving, helping and providing for your father and mother (cf. Ex 20:12). Suppose you are a prince, whose posterity will ensure peace to citizens of the crown and provide protection from tyranny, rebellion or civil war. . . . The opportunity of achieving such a great benefit binds you to beget lawful successors in a holy marriage. Here is no loss of chastity—or, at least, you surrender it chastely—if, for charity's sake, you sacrifice it to the public good. Suppose your health is poor, or uncertain; suppose you need much care and attention. . . . Do not deliberately commit yourself to actual poverty; charity forbids it.

Charity not only forbids fathers of families to sell all that belongs to them and give the money to the poor; it commands them to acquire honestly whatever is needed for the support of a wife and family, for the education of their children—just as it binds kings and princes to lay by financial resources (justly, not tyrannically, acquired) for the defense of the realm. Does not St. Paul advise married people (cf. 1 Cor 7:5), once the time for prayer is over, to come together again and resume their marital intercourse?

Counsels are given for the perfection of Christian people, but not for the perfection of each individual Christian. Circumstances make a counsel now impossible, now useless, now dangerous, now harmful to this or that individual. There you have the idea behind our Lord's words concerning one counsel—words he meant to be understood as referring to every counsel: *Take this in, you whose hearts are large enough for it* (Mt 19:12). It was as though he were saying, St. Jerome explains: "Take this in, you who value the honor of chastity to the extent of gaining it; it is offered to those who keep their hearts high." Not everyone can—should, I mean—always keep all the counsels. They are given for charity's sake; charity, then, is the rule and measure of their practice.

At charity's command, therefore, monks and friars are dragged from their cloisters to be created cardinals, turned prelates, or made parish priests; occasionally, even, they find themselves obliged to carry to win a kingdom's repose—as I have just mentioned. If charity can expel from the cloistered life such as have embraced it by solemn vow, we have all the more reason for appealing to the same authority when it comes to advising people to live at home, keep their property, marry, even join the armed forces and go to war despite its dangers.

Charity, when it calls some to a life of poverty or recalls others, when it impels some to marriage or others to continence, when it shuts the cloister door on one person and opens it to another, can never be called upon to give its reasons. Where the laws of Christianity are concerned, charity has fullness of power—for it is written: *charity sustains to the last* (1 Cor 13:7), never acts without reason. Call charity to account, demand the reason for its activities . . . fearlessly will come the answer: *The Lord has need of them* (Mt 21:3).

Charity is the motive and mainspring of all things, and God is the source of charity. Everything is at charity's service, but charity knows no master—not even God, for charity is bride not servant, engaged not in service but in love. That is why charity regulates the order in which the counsels are followed, why we take our cue from charity—chastity not poverty for this person, obedience not chastity for that one; fasting not almsgiving for these people, almsgiving not fasting for those; solitude not parochial duties for this individual, social life and not solitude for that one.

It comes to this: charity falls like dew from heaven upon the garden of the Church; it brings the flowers to life; it gives to each its color—the martyrs outshine the redness of any rose, the virgins outdo any lily in its whiteness. Some souls are dyed purple by mortification, others show the golden hue of marriage cares. The counsels are brought to bear in various ways upon the perfection of souls whose good fortune it is to live under charity's guidance.

(*Treatise* VIII, 6)

God's Will Declared through Inspirations

The sun's rays give both light and warmth together. Inspiration is a ray of grace bringing light and warmth to our hearts: light to show us what is good; warmth to give us energy to go after it. All living things in this world are numbed by winter's cold; with the return of spring's warmth they come to life again—animals move more swiftly, birds fly higher with livelier song, plants gaily bud and blossom. Without inspiration the life of the soul is sluggish, impotent, useless. Once the rays of God's inspirations strike it, however, we are aware of light and life . . . our minds are enlightened, our wills inflamed and quickened with strength to intend and fulfil whatever may lead to our salvation.

The ways he has of inspiring us are past all counting. Saints Anthony, Francis of Assisi, Anselm, and many others, often received inspirations while looking at creatures. Preaching, however, is the usual way; but occasionally those who are not helped by hearing the word are taught by trials. As the prophet said: *The very alarm of it will make you understand the revelation at last* (Is 28:19)—in other words, those who fail to amend their lives after hearing God's threats to the wicked will be taught the truth by the effects of some untoward event; the experience of misfortune will gain them wisdom. St. Mary of Egypt was inspired by seeing a picture of our Lady; St. Anthony by hearing the gospel read at Mass; St. Augustine by listening to a life of St. Anthony; the Duke of Gandia[1] by the sight of an empress' corpse; St. Pachomius by noticing an act of charity; the saintly Ignatius of Loyola by reading the lives of the saints. St. Cyprian (not the Bishop of Carthage, but a layman who was a glorious martyr) was touched at the sight of the devil admitting his impotence against those who trust in God.

Blessed are those whose hearts are ever open to God's inspiration; they will never lack what they need to live good holy lives, or to perform properly the duties of their state. For just as God gives each animal through its nature the instincts needed for its self-preservation and for the use of its natural powers, so—if we offer no obstacle to grace—he gives each of us the inspirations needed for life, activity and self-preservation on the spiritual level.

Most assuredly, souls who are not content with merely keeping the bridegroom's commands and counsels, but who readily follow his inspirations, are those whom the eternal Father has destined to be the brides of his beloved Son. Since Eliezer, for his part, had no other means of discovering which of the girls of Haran (the city where Nachor dwelt) was destined for his master's son, God revealed it to him by an inspiration.

---

1. St. Francis Borgia.

When we are at a loss what to do, when human help fails us in our dilemmas, then it is that God inspires us. If only we are humbly obedient, he will not let us go astray. But I will say no more about such necessary inspirations. I have frequently mentioned them in this volume, and also in my *Introduction to the Devout Life*.[1]

(*Treatise* VIII, 10)

To sum up what I have said about the union of the human will with God's declared will . . . Some plants point their flowers at the sun, turn them with it as it moves. The sunflower, however, turns not only its flowers, but its leaves as well. In the same way all God's chosen ones turn their hearts toward God's will by keeping his commandments. But those who are utterly filled with charity turn to God's will by more than mere obedience to his commandments; they also give him their hearts, follow him in all that he commands, counsels or inspires, unreservedly, with no exceptions whatever. Such souls are well able to echo the psalmist: *I was all dumbness, I was all ignorance, standing there like a brute beast in thy presence. Yet ever thou art at my side, ever holdest me by my right hand. Thine to guide me with thy counsel, thine to welcome me into glory at last* (Ps 72:22, 23).

(*Treatise* VIII, 13)

A Short Method of Knowing God's Declared Will

God's will is made known to us, says St. Basil, by what he disposes, what he commands. This calls for no deliberation on our part; we simply carry out God's orders. In everything else, however, we are perfectly free to make our own choice of what seems good—though it is not a question of doing everything that is permissible, but only such things as are suitable. To discover exactly what is appropriate, St. Basil concludes, we are to take the advice of a prudent spiritual director.

However, I have a warning for you, Theotimus. Souls who long to come as near as possible to God's will in everything often meet with a troublesome temptation. No matter what they are about, the devil raises

---

1. Part II, chapter 18.

doubts as to whether God wants them to do one thing rather than another. Is it God's will, for instance, to dine with a friend or not; to wear black or grey; to fast on a Friday or a Saturday; to enjoy oneself or not? Much time is lost in this way. While they busy or worry themselves trying to discover which is better, they miss the opportunity of doing much that is good. Deeds give God far more glory than any amount of time wasted in trying to discriminate between good and better.

We are not given to weighing tiny coins, only large ones. Trade would be troublesome and eat up too much time, if we had to weigh farthings and halfpennies. Neither are we to weigh every tiny action, to see if it is better than another; that way lies superstition. What good does it do to rack our brains over whether it is better to hear Mass in this church rather than that; whether to knit or sew; whether to give alms to a man or to a woman? To spend as much time reflecting on our duty as doing it is not the ideal way to serve a master. We must proportion our attention to the importance of the task at hand. To take as much trouble over making up our minds about going a short journey as about travelling a thousand miles or more would be conscientiousness run riot.

Choosing a vocation, planning something that is important, time-consuming or costly, moving house, making friends—things of that kind deserve serious reflection, to see where God's will chiefly lies. In tiny daily activities, however, where even a mistake is neither important nor irreparable, what need is there to make a fuss about them, or give them too much thought, or get in other people's way by seeking advice about them? What is the point of troubling myself to find out which God would prefer me to say—the rosary or the Little Office of our Lady? The difference between them is too slight for all that investigation. Should I visit the sick in the hospital or go to vespers? Should I listen to a sermon rather than visit a church where I could gain an indulgence? . . . There is nothing, normally, to show that one thing is so evidently superior to the other as to call for the making of great decisions. We are to go ahead simply and sincerely on such occasions, choosing what we think is good (as St. Basil says), without giving ourselves a headache, wasting our time, or laying ourselves open to the dangers of worry, scruples, superstition— always on the understanding, of course, that there is no great disparity between one thing and another, or no special considerations involved.

Even in spiritual matters we are to be very humble, nor are we to imagine that we can discover God's will by praying or by clever reasoning. First we must ask for light from the Holy Spirit, then concentrate on discovering God's permissive will, take the advice of our spiritual director and (if necessary) of two or three others, make up our minds, and come to a decision in God's name.

Afterwards we are not to question our choice, but devotedly, calmly, steadfastly keep it up, carry it through. Although difficulties, temptations and many different things may beset our path, to make us wonder if we have done right, we are to remain resolute and take no notice. Remember: had we made another choice, we might probably have found things a hundred times worse—to say nothing of the fact that we are in the dark as to whether God wishes us to experience comfort or trials, peace or war. Once our decision has been taken with God's help, we need never fear but that God will aid us to carry it through; as long as it does not depend on us, it cannot fail. To act in any other way is proof of excessive self-love, or of childishness, want of character, and sheer stupidity.

(*Treatise* VIII, 14)

By Way of Transition: An Early Memo[1]

Everyone is obliged to strive for the perfection of Christian life, because our Lord commands that we be perfect and St. Paul says the same (Mt 5:48; 2 Cor 13:11). Perfection of Christian life consists in conforming our wills to that of our good God, who is the sovereign standard and norm for all actions. So in order to acquire perfection we must always consider and recognize what God's will is in everything that concerns us, so that we can flee what He wants us to avoid and accomplish what He wants us to do.

There are some matters in which it is clear what God's will is, as in what concerns the commandments or the duties of one's vocation. That is why we must always seek to carry out well what God expects of all Christians, as well as what our own vocation requires of us in particular. Anyone who does not do this much with care can possess nothing but a fraudulent devotion.

There are still other matters about which there is no doubt whether God

---

1. *Oeuvres* XXVI, 185-87. Francis would occasionally draft short memos on basic topics which could circulate among several of his directees. This memo, though not complete, is an interesting example of the genre.

wills them, such as trials, illnesses and chronic conditions. That is why
we should accept them with a good heart, and conform our will to that of
God who permits them. Anyone who can arrive at the point of not only
supporting them patiently but even of willing them, that person can be
said to have acquired a great conformity. Thus, the death of relatives,
various losses, illnesses, dryness or distractions in prayer—these give us
opportunities to grow in perfection.

But we must go further and see this will not only in great afflictions
but even in little reversals and minor inconveniences that we will always
meet with in this unhappy life.

In this regard many people make a mistake because they prepare
themselves only for major afflictions and remain totally without defense,
strength or resistance when it comes to small ones. Actually it would be
more understandable to be less prepared for major afflictions which
happen but rarely, and to be prepared for the little ones which come up
every day and at every moment. I will give you an example of what I
mean: I prepare myself to suffer death patiently—which can happen to
me but once—and I do not prepare myself at all to put up with the
inconveniences I encounter from the moods of those I am with, or the
pressing spiritual demands which my work brings me and which arise a
hundred times a day. And that is what makes me imperfect.

There are many other things I am not obliged to do either by the general
commandments of God or by the duties of my own vocation, and with
these it is necessary to consider carefully in liberty of spirit what would
tend to the greatest glory of God, because that is what God wills. I said
"in liberty of spirit" because this should be done without pressure or
anxiety, but by a simple glance at the good which our action can produce,
such as, for example, to make a short pilgrimage, to go to confession, to
visit a sick person, to give a small sum for the love of God. If it is not a
matter of great importance, then we should not invest a great concern in
it, but after a little thought we must decide. And if afterward the action
or the decision doesn't seem good, and it looks as if I had made a mistake,
I should in no way blame or bother myself about it, but rather humble
myself and laugh at myself.

But if it is a matter of importance, like changing one's profession,
making final vows, undertaking a long voyage, or giving a great sum of
money to charity—after having thought about it for a while, we must
confer with the spiritual persons to whom we look for direction, and go
along with their advice with simplicity, for God will assist them to direct

us rightly. And if through their fault the decision is not the best in itself, that won't prevent it from being the most useful and meritorious for you, for God will render it fruitful.[1]

(Letters, pp. 105-06)

The Will of God's Good Pleasure, or "Permissive Will"

Sin excepted, nothing happens but by God's will—by a positive or permissive will which no one can obstruct, which is known only by its results. These events, when they occur, show us that God has willed and planned them.

If we reflect here and now on everything that was, is, or ever will be, we shall be lost in wonderment, forced to echo the psalmist's cry: *Lord, I praise thee for my wondrous fashioning, for all the wonders of thy creation. Of my soul thou hast full knowledge . . . such wisdom as thine is far beyond my reach, no thought of mine can attain it* (Ps 138:14, 6). From that we pass to gratification, to delight that God is infinite in wisdom, power and goodness. The universe is but a tiny sample, a showcase, as it were, of these three divine attributes.

Come, at last, to our own selves. Ponder our many blessings of soul and body, also the mental and physical sufferings providence has in store for us. Let us open the arms of our assent, let us clasp all these things in a loving embrace, let us comply with God's holy will—these words the eternal hymn upon our lips: *Thy will be done, on earth as it is in heaven* (Mt 6:10). Yes, Lord, *thy will be done on earth*—where we know no pleasure untinged by pain, no roses without thorns, no day unclosed by night, no spring but winter goes before; *on earth,* Lord—where comforts are few, where toils are many. For all that, O God, *thy will be done*—not only in the keeping of your commandments, counsels, inspirations, where we are active, but also in the enduring of suffering and sorrow, where we are passive. So may your will do by us, for us, in us, with us, all it pleases.

(Treatise IX, 1)

---

1. The manuscript breaks off in the middle of the next paragraph. Compare this early text with the *Treatise on the Love of God* VIII and IX, especially VIII, 14 (*Oeuvres* V, 105-07).

Seen Especially in Trials and Difficulties

There is nothing attractive about trials in themselves; only when seen as coming from providence, enjoined by God's will, are they infinitely lovable. On the ground Moses' staff was a frightful serpent; in his hand it was a miraculous wand (cf. Ex 7). Trials, in themselves, are dreadful; seen as part of God's will, they are attractive, delightful. Nothing is commoner than to experience reluctance at taking remedies prescribed and administered by a doctor; yet, were they to come from someone we love, we should take them gladly—love conquering disgust. Love either rids work of its disagreeableness or renders our experience of it pleasant; that is certain. They tell of a river in Boeotia where the fish seem to be golden; take them out of their native element, they are like any other fish. So it is with things that distress us: if we divorce them from God's will, they are naturally unpleasant; if we see them as part of God's eternal permissive will, they are perfectly golden, lovable, unspeakably precious.

If the martyrs had failed to see God's permissive will in their tortures, how could they have broken into song in face of dungeon, fire and sword? The person who truly loves God loves the divine permissive will when things go badly no less than if they go well. In fact his or her love for God's will is greater amid crosses, toil and trouble; love chiefly shows itself in suffering for the one we love.

To love God's will when all goes well is to love aright, as long as we really do love his will and not the comfortable effects of it. Nevertheless, it is a love that knows no opposition, no reluctance, no effort; surely anyone would love a will so deserving of love, so attractively portrayed. To love God's will in his commandments, counsels, inspirations, is a stage higher, much more perfect. This leads us to give up and forgo our own wills, our own desires, so that we deprive ourselves of pleasure up to a point. To love suffering and distress out of love for God is charity's highest degree.

The traveler afraid of missing his way takes uncertain steps, scanning his surroundings, stopping at every turning to make sure he has not gone astray; the person who is sure of his route makes his way cheerfully, fearlessly, briskly. It is exactly the same with love that would reach God's will by way of consolations—it is ever afraid of taking the wrong path, of loving the delight it experiences rather than the fact that it is God's delight to afford it. However, love that moves toward God's will through distress feels secure; there is nothing attractive about distress, so there is no difficulty in loving it only because God sends it.

In springtime hounds are constantly at a loss, apparently lacking all sense of smell, because the scent of fields and flowers is stronger than that of hart or hare. Amid the springtime of consolations love is but dimly aware of what pleases God, since the sense pleasure afforded by consolation distracts attention from the will of God. When our Lord offered St. Catherine of Siena the choice of two crowns, one of gold and one of thorns, she chose the crown of thorns as more in keeping with love. Choosing to suffer, said the saintly Angela of Foligno, is a certain proof of love; while St. Paul declared that he would not *make a display of anything, except the cross* (Gal 6:14; 2 Cor 12:5, 10), except the weaknesses that humiliated him, except the persecutions he underwent for Christ.

(*Treatise* IX, 2)

Accepted through Resignation or "Deference"

The highest, purest test of love is undoubtedly inward assent to the trials of the spiritual life. The saintly Angela of Foligno gives a wonderful description of the inner anguish she sometimes felt. Her soul suffered, she says, "like a person bound hand and foot hanging by the neck, half strangled, between life and death, all hope of rescue lost"—unable to put foot to ground, use her hands, cry for help, scarcely able to breathe or moan. That is how it is, Theotimus. There are times when our souls are harassed to such an extent by inward trials that all their powers and faculties are deadened through being deprived of all possible relief, through being aware and afraid of all possible discouragement. After our Savior's example, we begin to grow dismayed and distressed like a person in his or her last moments, until we can truthfully echo our Lord's cry: *My soul is ready to die with sorrow* (Mk 14:33, 34; Mt 26:37-39). Deep down inside ourselves we are led to wish, to plead that *if it were possible, this chalice might pass us by.* The soul's very peak, its apex, alone remains riveted to God's love, to his permissive will, in simple submission: *Only as thy will is,* eternal Father, *not as mine is* (Lk 22:42).

What is important is the fact that we make this act of deference to God's will in the face of so much difficulty, so many obstacles, so much reluctance, that we are scarcely aware of making it. At least it seems so cold and lifeless as to be made grudgingly, unbecomingly. Doing God's will, at times like these, not only lacks all pleasure, all contentment, but it goes against all our inclinations, all our self-satisfaction. Love lets the heart lament (where lament it must), lets it rehearse all the lamentations that fell from the lips of Job or Jeremiah—on condition, however, that the virtue of submission be practiced deep in the soul, at its apex, its noblest and highest part.

There is nothing loving or peaceful about such submission; genuine, steady, indomitable and heartfelt though it is, it can be scarcely felt. It seems to withdraw to the very core of the soul, the center of the citadel, where it stands its ground, though all around is unrest, unhappiness. The more such circumstances deprive love of all encouragement, cut short all assistance to the soul's powers and faculties, the more credit it deserves for remaining so staunchly faithful.

Such union, such compliance with God's permissive will, is achieved either by the virtue of deference or by the more perfect virtue of disinterestedness. The practice of deference involves effort, involves submission. Life is preferable to death, for instance; but we defer to death because God permits it. We would rather live, if that met with God's approval; in fact we turn to him for length of life. We may be ready to die, but we have a much greater readiness to live; we may depart this world submissively enough, but we would be much happier to remain. Job, in his troubles, practiced deference: *What, should we accept the good fortune God sends us, and not the ill?* (Jb 2:10). Note that he speaks of accepting—of enduring or putting up with something. *Nothing is here befallen but what was the Lord's will; blessed be the name of the Lord* (Jb 1:21)—that is deference, that is acceptance speaking, patient under suffering.

(*Treatise* IX, 3)

Embracing the Will of God's Good Pleasure by "Disinterested Love"

Deference means that we prefer God's will to all else, though we know a great attraction to many other things. Disinterestedness is a stage higher—it means that we are lovingly attracted to a thing only because we see God's will in it; nothing else interests the unencumbered heart, when God's will makes itself felt.

If all I want is a drink of water, do I mind whether it is in a golden goblet or a plain glass? Does it really matter, then, how God's will is presented to me, since it is equally present in misfortune or consolation? I should probably prefer the plain glass, to see the water. . . . God's will is never clearer than when there is no distracting beauty about the way it comes.

Beyond compare is St. Paul; his disinterestedness surpasses the heroic. *I am hemmed in on both sides,* he tells the Philippians. *I long to have done with this life, and be with Christ, a better thing, much more than a better thing; and yet, for your sakes, that I should wait in the body is more urgent still* (Phil 1:23, 24). That great bishop, St. Martin, followed the apostle's example. At the close of his life he longed to go home to God, yet indicated his willingness to continue working for the good of his flock. These words were on his lips:

> *How lovely is your dwelling place,*
> *O Lord of hosts.*
> *My soul is longing and yearning,*
> *is yearning for the courts of the Lord.*
> *My heart and my soul ring out their joy*
> *to God, the living God.*   (Ps 83:1-3)

Yet he went on to exclaim: "Nevertheless, Lord, if I am still needed here for the salvation of souls, it is not for me to lay down the burden; *thy will be done* (Mt 6:10)."

How wonderful it was!—the loving self-surrender of the apostle and of that apostolic man. Before them they saw the open gates of heaven or the myriad toils of earth. No thoughts of self-interest dictated their choice; only God's will could sway their hearts. The joys of heaven are not a whit preferable to the sorrows of this world, if God's permissive will has an equal place in both. Toil is heavenly if that is God's will; heaven would be wearisome were it not God's will. The whole longing of heaven and earth (as David says) is for God's will to be done: *What else does heaven hold for me,* Lord, *but thyself? What charm for me has earth, here at thy side?* (Ps 72:25).

The heart of a disinterested person is like wax in God's hands, ready for every impression of the eternal will. Such a heart knows no personal preference, equally prepared for anything, its one aim the fulfilling of God's will. It is not attracted by the things God wants, only by his will that wants them.

(*Treatise* IX, 4)

Disinterestedness is to be shown in natural things, such as health, sickness, beauty, plainness, weakness, strength; in social life, such as honors, rank, or wealth; in the ebb and flow of the spiritual life, such as dryness, encouragement, enthusiasm, boredom; in activity, in suffering— in a word, in whatever happens.

Job, in his natural life, was smitten with foulest scab from head to foot; in his social life he was mocked, baited, blamed—even by those nearest to him; in his spiritual life he was crushed by apathy, exhaustion, turmoil, anguish, darkness and every kind of unbearable inner torment, as his plaints and sighs gave proof.

St. Paul exhorts us to complete disinterestedness in all things, to show that we are God's true servants. . . . We have to show great patience, in times of affliction, of need, of difficulty; under the lash, in prison, in the midst of tumult; when we are tired out, sleepless, and fasting. We have to be pure-minded, enlightened, forgiving and gracious to others; we have to rely on the Holy Spirit, on unaffected love, on the truth of our message, on the power of God. To right and to left we must be armed with innocence; now honored, now slighted, now traduced, now flattered. They call us deceivers, and we tell the truth; unknown, and we are fully acknowledged; dying men, and see, we live; punished, yes, but not doomed to die; sad men, that rejoice continually; beggars, that bring riches to many; disinherited, and the world is ours (2 Cor 6:4-10).

I would have you notice, Theotimus, how distressing was the life of an apostle: physically, *under the lash;* socially, *in prison, traduced.* Such people showed a disinterested love, God knows! They were joyful in their sorrows, rich in their poverty; their deaths were life-giving, their disrepute a claim to renown. They were glad to be sad, content to be poor, gained new life when death threatened, found fame in being slighted—for such was God's will. Because God's will is more evident in suffering than in the practice of any other virtue, St. Paul gives patience the first place: *We have to show great patience, in times of affliction, of need, of difficulty.* Only later does he go on to say: *We have to be pure-minded, enlightened, forgiving and gracious to others.*

Our Savior too knew distress beyond compare in his social life on earth: he was condemned for treason against God and humanity; he was struck, scourged, mocked and tortured with unusual shame. In his natural life he died under the cruellest, most agonizing punishment imaginable. In his spiritual life he suffered sadness, fear, dismay, anguish, abandonment, weariness of soul—the like of which had never been known, nor will be again. He experienced the full enjoyment of eternal glory in the highest part of his human soul, it is true; yet love barred this glory from shedding its delights over feelings, over imagination, over passions, thus leaving our Lord's heart a prey to sorrow, to anguish.

To Ezekiel *it seemed as if an outstretched hand caught* him by a lock of his hair; and with that, a force lifted him *up between heaven and earth* (Ez 8:3). Does it not seem as though our Lord, lifted up between heaven and earth on the cross, were held in his Father's hand by a single hair, by the apex of his soul, which alone knew the fullness of bliss? Sadness and weariness engulfed the rest of his soul, so that he exclaimed: *My God, my God, why hast thou forsaken me?* (Mt 27:46).

A fish called "sea-lantern" is said to thrust its tongue out of the water at the height of a storm. So bright and clear is the tongue's glow, it serves as flare or beacon to sailors. When our Lord was submerged in a sea of passions, all his soul's faculties were overwhelmed, buried in stormy waves of suffering—all except the soul's highest point, trouble-free, bright, shining with bliss and glory. Blessed, indeed, is charity; it reigns in the apex of any faithful soul submerged by the waves and breakers of inner trials.

(*Treatise* IX, 5)

Things that happen are the almost exclusive means of recognizing God's positive or permissive will. As long as we are unaware of what God wants here and now, we must cling as closely as possible to his declared will, which has been revealed to us. But the moment it becomes apparent what God wants of us, we must immediately fall in with it, obey it lovingly.

My mother or myself (it makes no difference) is ill in bed; how can I tell whether or not God means the sickness to be fatal? I am completely in the dark, that is certain. But this I do know: while I await the outcome allotted by his permissive will, he intends me—by his declared will—to do everything possible to get well, as conscientiously as I can. However, if God's will permits the disease to get the better of the remedies, and end in death, then, as soon as the event vouches for it, I shall lovingly comply in the apex of my soul, whatever reluctance I may feel in the lower part. *"Be it so,* Lord,"I shall murmur; "I am quite willing, *since this finds favor in thy sight* (Mt 11:26). So it has appealed to you, now it is to my liking too—your will's humble servant."

The fact is that God often fires us with ambitious aims, which he does not mean to succeed, so as to furnish us with a chance of displaying the virtue of perfect disinterestedness. When this happens, not only are we to take up and carry out the work at hand as boldly, bravely and steadfastly as we can, but also we are to accept meekly and calmly whatever outcome God sees fit to send. St. Louis was inspired to cross the seas and win back the holy land; it turned out otherwise, and he meekly accepted the reverse. His calm submission means more to me than his high-souled resolve. St. Francis of Assisi made his way to Egypt, to convert the infidels or to win martyrdom from them; such was God's will. Yet Francis came home again with neither aim accomplished; and that too was God's will. It was equally God's will that St. Anthony of Padua should desire martyrdom, and that he should not gain it. It was no small task for the saintly Ignatius of Loyola to set on foot the Society of Jesus. He saw it do great things, and he foresaw even greater in the future; yet he had the courage to resolve that, should he see it disbanded—the keenest disappointment he could experience—within half an hour he would be unwaveringly at peace with God's will. Andalusia's learned and saintly preacher, John of Avila, planned to form a society of model priests to work for God's greater glory. He had gone some way toward achieving this, when he noticed the Jesuits were pursuing the same object. This appeared to be sufficient for the needs of the day, so he cut short his own scheme with a meekness and humility beyond compare.

Blessed, indeed, are souls like that; they are dauntless and sturdy in undertaking whatever God inspires, docile and submissive in giving it up whenever God desires. There you have the characteristic features of disinterestedness at its highest—to leave off doing a good thing when God sees fit, to stop half-way when God's will (our guide) enjoins it.

Most assuredly, Jonah was wrong to take it amiss when, as far as he could see, God failed to fulfil his prophecy of doom against Nineveh (cf. Jon 4:1). By foretelling the destruction of Nineveh Jonah did God's will; but he became personally concerned, entangled his own will with God's. That is why he was angry, and grumbled scandalously, when he saw that God did not fulfil his prophecy to the letter as he had proclaimed it. Had God's will, what the Lord wanted, been the only motive of Jonah's actions, he would have been just as happy to see it fulfilled in sparing Nineveh its threatened punishment as to see it satisfied by the avenging of Nineveh's crimes. Whatever we undertake or handle, we want it to succeed; but we cannot reasonably expect God to do everything to our liking. If God intended Nineveh to be threatened, but not overthrown— since a threat was sufficient to bring amendment—what cause had Jonah for complaint?

If that is the way of it, though, there would seem to be no call for us to bother about anything; we should just leave matters to the mercy of events. Forgive me, no. We are to overlook nothing that can contribute to the success of whatever it is to which God has set our hands; but on one condition—that, if the result is unfavorable, we accept it meekly and calmly. While we are commanded to take great care over what concerns God's glory and our duty, we are not held responsible for the outcome; there is nothing we can do about that. *Take care of him,* the inn-keeper was told, in the parable of the poor man half dead on the road between Jerusalem and Jericho (cf. Lk 10:30-35). "He was not told," comments St. Bernard, "to cure him." So it was that the apostles lovingly preached God's word to the Jews first, though they knew that eventually they would have to give it up as fruitless, and turn their thoughts to the Gentiles (cf. Acts 13:46, 47). It is for us to plant the seed, to water it carefully; only God can give the increase (cf. 1 Cor 3:6).

(*Treatise* IX, 6)

God has laid upon us the obligation of doing all we can to acquire virtue, so let us overlook nothing that may ensure success. But after we have planted and watered, let us be aware that it is God who gives the increase to our good tendencies and habits (cf. 1 Cor 3:6). That is why we are to look to his providence for the harvest of our desires and efforts. If we feel that we are not growing or advancing in devotion as well as we should wish, let us not upset ourselves, but be at peace, never traitors to tranquility of heart. Ours is the task of tilling the garden of our souls, so we must be faithful in devoting all our attention to it; abundance of crop and harvest we are to leave in our Lord's care. The ploughman will never be taken to task for not having a good harvest; only for not tilling his fields, for not sowing his seed.

Let us not be disconcerted at finding that we are always novices in the practice of virtue. Devotion is a monastery where each soul never thinks of itself but as a novice, where the whole of life is a time of trial. There is no clearer proof that we are not merely novices, but even deserving of dismissal, than to imagine that we are professed. The rules of this order are such that it is the keeping of the vows, not the making of them, which confers profession; nor is the practice of the vows ever complete, while opportunity of keeping them remains—and only death puts an end to the obligation of serving God, of growing in charity.

But wait, it may be objected: if I know that my slow rate of progress in practicing the virtues is due to my own fault, how can I help being dismayed, disturbed? I have already answered this in my *Introduction to the Devout Life*[1] but I gladly repeat it here; it can never be said too often. We are to be sorry for the sins we have committed, but our contrition is to be powerful, solid, steadfast, peaceful; it is not to be wild, uneasy, despondent. You admit to lagging on the path of virtue through your own fault. Come, then! Abase yourself in God's sight; beg his clemency; bow down and crave his pardon; confess your sin, cry mercy in the ear of your confessor, so as to win absolution. But this done, be at peace. Hate your sin, but love the humiliation you will feel at having made so little spiritual progress.

Take that good person over there who really wants, really tries to rid himself of a tendency to anger. In this he has had the help of God's grace; it has set him free from all sins due to anger. That person would rather die than utter an insulting word or show the slightest sign of hatred. Yet he is still a prey to the onset, the initial impulses of that passion—to those stirrings, disturbances, flashes of anger in the heart to which the psalmist

---

1.   Part III, chapter 9.

is referring when he says: *Tremble, and sin no more* (Ps 4:5)—sometimes translated as: "Be angry, and sin not." It comes to the same thing: if we are surprised into anger, experiencing the first tremblings of fury in our hearts, we are to be very careful not to let ourselves be carried away—otherwise we should sin. There is nothing sinful about these initial stirrings or tremblings of anger, yet the unfortunate soul that is often seized by them becomes agitated, frets and worries; it even thinks its dismay is a good thing brought on by the love of God. Nevertheless, this agitation is not the work of charity, which only takes offence at sin; it is prompted by self-love, which would have us exempt from the anguish, the effort, to which the onset of anger gives rise. No fault annoys us in these stirrings of anger, for there is no sin in them at all; what disturbs us is the difficulty of holding out against them.

Indeed, as I have pointed out earlier,[1] the Church condemned the false notion of certain hermits who taught that we could be entirely exempt in this world from passions of anger, concupiscence, fear, and the like. God means us to have enemies; he means us to repulse them. Let us bear ourselves bravely between these two aspects of God's will—patient when we are beset, courageous when we stand at bay.

(*Treatise* IX, 7)

God knows an utter hatred of sin; yet, in his great wisdom, he permits it. He does so to allow rational creatures to act in accord with their natures; also to make those who are good more praiseworthy for doing no wrong, when wrong lay in their power. It is for us, then, to adore and praise God's permissive will. However, since providence has an infinite hatred of the sin it permits, we are to share that hatred; it is for us to wish with all our might that sin permitted may never be sin committed. Consequently, we are to make use of every possible means to prevent sin coming to birth, growing, and tyrannizing us. In this we are to imitate our Lord, who never ceases to urge, promise, threaten, forbid, command or inspire us, in order to turn our wills away from sin—as far as that is possible without destroying our freedom.

But if sin has been committed, let us do all we can to wipe it out. Our

---

1. Book I, chapter 3.

Lord was ready to do this, he assured Carpus (as I have already mentioned[1]); he was ready to submit to death all over again, if need be, in order to release a single soul from sin. If the sinner persists in evil ways, let us weep, Theotimus, let us sigh and pray for that sinner to the Savior of our souls.

Still, however stubborn sinners may be, we are not to lose heart in coming to their aid, in doing what we can for them. For all we know, they may do penance and be saved. Well for you, if you can say to your neighbors, like St. Paul: *Do not forget the three years I spent, instructing every one of you continually, and with tears* (Acts 20:31). *And I ask you to bear me witness today that I have no man's blood on my hands; I have never shrunk from revealing to you the whole of God's plan* (Acts 20:27). As long as there is any chance of a sinner mending his ways (and while there is life, there is hope), we are never to dismiss him, but go on praying for him, giving him what help his sorry state allows.

But at long last, after we have wept over the stubborn, after we have tried to save them in charity, we are to imitate our Lord and the apostles; in other words, we are to turn our minds to other things, other activities more conducive to God's glory.

(Treatise IX, 8)

Disinterested Love Exercised in Prayer

One of the finest musicians this world has known, a marvelous lute player, in a short time went stone deaf. He still continued to sing, however, and to finger his lute with wondrous delicacy, for deafness did not deprive him of his long-accustomed skill. But, because he could not hear, neither song nor lute could please him. For this reason he sang and played only to satisfy a prince with whom he had been brought up as a child. Nothing pleased the musician more than to please the prince, to win from him appreciation of a song. Yet sometimes, to prove the musician's love, the prince would tell him to sing, then leave him for the hunting-field. On and on would sing the other, as though his master were still there; no

---

1.   Book VIII, chapter 4.

pleasure in it for himself—his deafness deprived him of the enjoyment of melody, his master's absence took away the satisfaction of making the prince happy.

A true heart, my God, a heart true to thy service; its song, its music are for thee! Wake, my soul, wake, echoes of harp and viol; dawn shall find me watching (Ps 56:8:9). The human heart, after all, is charity's chorister; it is harp and viol too. Usually this chorister hears his own voice, enjoys listening to the melody of his own song; in other words, the human heart enjoys its love for God, utterly content to love what is so lovable.

Do you see what I mean? Young nightingales learn to sing by imitating older ones; but once they have mastered the art, they sing for the sheer joy of warbling and become so fond of their delight that, as I have said elsewhere, they shatter their throats with strain of singing, and die.[1] Our hearts in the same way, at the threshold of devotion, love God in order to become one with him, pleasing to him, and to imitate his eternal love for us. But perhaps gradually, as we grow in charity, there is an imperceptible change of heart: instead of loving God to please him, we begin to love for the pleasure we feel; instead of falling in love with God, we fall in love with our love for him. We are partial to our own fancies; we no longer enjoy God, but the pleasure we find in loving him. What satisfies us is that it is *our* love, something that belongs to us, comes from us; although we call it the love of God, because he is the one we love, it is really ours, for we are the lovers.

This is how the change occurs: instead of loving charity because it leads to God whom we love, we love it because it wells up in us who are the lovers. Don't you see that by so doing we no longer seek God? We have come back to ourselves—in love with love, not the beloved. We are in love with love, I repeat, not because it gratifies God's wishes, but because it is a source of satisfaction to ourselves. Thus the chorister who began by singing to and for God is now rather singing to and for himself; if he enjoys singing, it is not so much to please God's ear as his own. The song of charity is the best song of all, so the chorister loves it most—only not because it is in praise of God's greatness, but because it has a more satisfying, more attractive melody.

(*Treatise* IX, 9)

---

1.   *Treatise* V, 8.

You will recognize it all right, Theotimus. If the mystic nightingale sings to please God, it will sing the song it knows God likes; but if it sings to please itself, it will sing what takes its own fancy, what it thinks will give self the most pleasure. Take two divine songs; one could be sung because it is divine, the other because it is pleasing. Rachel and Leah were equally Jacob's wives; but one was loved merely as a wife, the other also for her beauty. The song may be God's, but the motive for singing it could be the spiritual gratification we expect from it.

"Don't you see," you could say to me, "that God means you to sing the pastoral song of his love to your people? In charity's name he commands you three times to feed your flock, speaking to you through St. Peter (cf. Jn 21:15-17), the first pastor. What's that you say? Rome or Paris offers greater spiritual consolations; charity is easier to practice there!" Heaven knows, if that were so, I should not be singing to please God, but myself; I should not be seeking God through charity, but the personal gratification which the practice of charity brings!

Religious priests would like to sing the song of secular priests, married folk the song of religious; they mean by it, they say, to love and serve God better. Why, you are deceiving yourselves, my friends; don't say it is to love and serve God better. Of course not; it is to minister more to your own satisfaction, which you prefer to God's. In health or sickness we can find God's will—usually more so in sickness; but if we prefer health, let us not pretend that this is the better way to serve God. Can't you see that all we want from God's will is health? We are not really trying to see health as something God wills.

It is difficult, I admit, to enjoy looking at a beautiful mirror for very long without catching sight of ourselves, and liking that. It is also difficult, of course, to love God and not love too the pleasures this gives us. But there is all the difference between the joy we take in loving God because his beauty attracts us, and the joy we take in loving God because we find it pleasant. Our aim must be to love God for his beauty, not to enjoy the beauty of loving him.

At prayer, if you are aware that you are praying, your attention has wandered; you have taken your mind away from God to let it rest upon what you are doing. Our biggest distraction, very often, is the care we take not to have any distractions! Simplicity is the best way in spiritual things. If you want to contemplate God—do that, and don't think of anything else. If you begin to look back on yourself, to examine your contemplation, you are no longer looking at God, but at your own behavior, yourself. We are praying fervently, if we cannot tell whether we are praying or not; we are not concerned with what we are doing, all our thoughts are on God. If we are afire with charity we are not constantly examining our conscience; we keep ourselves preoccupied with the God we love. The heavenly chorister so enjoys giving God pleasure that the only enjoyment he finds in his own melodious voice is the pleasure it affords God.

Look at that man over there, saying his prayers; he seems to be so devoted, so on fire with charity. Wait a while, however, and you will see if it is God he loves. As soon as the charm and gratification which he feels in loving come to an end, as soon as dryness appears, he will not keep it up, but only pray occasionally. Had it been God he was loving, why did he stop? After all, God is still God. It was the encouragement which God gives that he was in love with, not *the God who gives all encouragement* (2 Cor 1:3).

Most assuredly, many people have no time for loving God unless the process is steeped in sense pleasure; like children given bread and honey, they would like to lick off the honey and leave the bread. If they could separate love from the pleasure of loving, they would throw away the love and keep the pleasure. This means that since they follow love because it is pleasant, once they find nothing in it any more, they have no further time for it. Such folk are in grave danger of either turning back when encouragement fails, when inclination flags, or of wasting time over false charms which bear no relation to true love—and, seeking honey, catch the bee by the tail.

(*Treatise* IX, 10)

The musician I mentioned found no satisfaction in singing, after he became deaf, except when he was aware that his prince was listening and enjoying it. Blessed indeed is the heart that loves God for the sole pleasure of pleasing God! What purer, more perfect happiness can you know than the happiness of pleasing the Godhead. To put it plainly, however, the delight of pleasing God is not exactly loving God; it is merely the result, the fruit of it; delight is as distinct from love as lemons from a lemon-tree. Our musician, as I told you, never enjoyed his own singing; his deafness prevented it. Often he also sang without the delight of pleasing his prince, who would go hunting after asking him to perform, no time or wish to listen.

Dear God, as long as I feel that you are pleased with my love song, how happy I am! Can any pleasure equal the delight of genuinely pleasing God? But when I am no longer aware of your gratification at my song—heaven knows, my soul is deeply troubled! Yet I go on loving you loyally, singing continually my chosen hymn. *I* don't benefit; my song gives *me* no pleasure; I sing it purely out of love for your will.

So it sometimes happens that we draw no comfort from practicing charity; like deaf choristers we are unable to hear our own voices, unable to enjoy the sweetness of our song. But this is not all: we are also harassed by many a fear, unsettled by the devil's disturbing influence on our hearts. He suggests that we do not win our Master's approval, that our love is useless, even insincere and empty, since it yields no comfort. Why then, not only is there no pleasure in our activity, but it becomes extremely wearisome; we see neither the good of what we do, nor the gratification of God for whom our work is done.

What makes matters worse, of course, is that the mind—at reason's highest point—can offer no sort of relief. Even the higher part of reason is beset by suggestions from the devil. It is utterly disturbed, busily engaged in trying to avoid being caught off balance and tricked into giving way to evil, so it cannot come to the relief of the mind's lower part. Even though we have not lost heart, the siege is desperate; free from guilt we may be, but not free from grief. To crown everything, we are deprived of the usual consolation we can fall back on when things go wrong in this world—the hope that they will not last long, but soon come to an end. In all these vexations of spirit we become practically incapable of even imagining they could end, and so fail to feel the comforting presence of hope. Faith, it is true, from its place in the apex of human reason, gives us complete assurance that the disturbance will cease, that we shall know peace at last. But the devil causes so great a disturbance in the rest of the soul, in the lower part of the reason, that he makes it almost impossible for faith's counsels and reproofs to be heard. Foreboding alone fills the imagination: "Happiness is not for me . . . ever."

Of all times, Theotimus, it is then that we must show invincible loyalty to our Savior; it is then that we must serve him purely out of love for his will—not only without pleasure, but overwhelmed by gloom, disgust, dread, and assailed by temptations. This is how it was with his glorious Mother and St. John on the day of the passion: in spite of all the blasphemies around them, all the anguish, all the distress of death, they stood resolute in love. So they stood even when the Savior, the beatific vision confined to the apex of his soul, allowed no sign of joy or comfort to spread over his features; when his eyes began to close, veiled by the shadows of death, filled with pain—darkened and terrible like the sun.

(Treatise IX, 11)

The Passing-Over of the Will

As St. Peter lay in prison awaiting martyrdom the following day, an angel visited him during the night and filled his cell with splendor (cf. Acts 12:6-11). He awoke the apostle, made him rise, gird himself, put on shoes and cloak. Then the angel struck off chains and manacles, and led Peter out of the prison. *Thus they passed one party of guards, then a second, and reached the iron gate which leads out into the city; this opened for them of its own accord. They came out, and as soon as they had passed up one street, the angel left him*—a free man. There you have a number of very real actions; yet Peter, awake from the beginning, was *unaware that what the angel had done for him was true; he thought he was seeing a vision.* He seemed unconscious of being awake, of dressing, of walking, of being freed. So great was the wonder of his rescue, it filled his mind to such an extent that, though he was quite aware of what he was doing, he could not believe it was actually true. He saw the angel well enough, but he could not tell that he was using his natural sight. That was why his rescue brought him no comfort until he came to himself later: *Now I can tell for certain, he said, that the Lord has sent his angel, to deliver me out of Herod's hands, and from all that the people of the Jews hoped to see.*

This is exactly what happens when people are weighed down by inner trials. Though they are quite capable of believing in, hoping in, and loving God; though they actually do so—yet they are too weak to be aware of it. So powerfully does their distress engross and overwhelm them, they cannot come to themselves, to see what they are about. For this reason they imagine they have neither faith, hope, nor charity, but only shadows, useless impressions of these virtues, which they feel almost without being aware of them, which seem foreign, not familiar to their souls.

If you watch out for it, you will find that our minds are in a similar state whenever they are powerfully preoccupied by some violent passion; we do a lot of things like people in a dream, so little aware of what we do that we are not really sure that it happens. That is why the psalmist described the great comfort experienced by the Israelites on their return from the Babylonian captivity in these words:

> When the Lord delivered Sion from bondage,
>   it seemed like a dream.
> Then was our mind filled with laughter,
>   on our lips there were songs.   (Ps 125:1)

Or, as the Vulgate (following the Septuagint) has it: *we became like people comforted.* In other words: the wonder of our good fortune was so tremendous that we could hardly feel the comfort it gave us. We almost believed that we had no comfort, that it was not actually happening to us, that it was only a symbol, a dream.

This is the sort of thing the soul goes through in the event of spiritual distress. Such experience makes love more genuine, more sincere; by taking away the pleasure which could rivet us to God, it joins and unites us to God directly, will to will, heart to heart, with no intervention of gratification or anticipated reward. Yet how distressful for the heart of a person, seemingly forsaken by love, to seek it everywhere and apparently fail to discover it. It is not to be found in the external senses, for they are not capable of it; nor in the imagination, cruelly harassed by conflicting impressions; nor in the judgment, disturbed by cloudy reasoning and strange fears. Although it is to be found eventually in the apex, the highest part of the soul, where charity has its dwelling-place, it is not recognized, does not appear to be love, since excessive weariness and gloom prevent experience of its charm. Such a person is unconsciously aware of it, unknowingly face to face with it—like a person in a dream, or seeing a vision. So it was that Mary Magdalen, when she met her Master, drew no comfort from his presence; she had no idea that it was he, but thought she was merely looking at the gardener (cf. Jn 20:15).

What is one to do in these circumstances? The soul can no longer bear up under such distress; all it can bring itself to do is let its will expire in the hands of God's will, in imitation of our gentle Jesus. When his sufferings on the cross reached the limits appointed by the Father, when he could no longer endure the intensity of his torments, he imitated the deer—out of breath and pursued by the pack, it surrenders to the hunter, its eyes filled with tears, a final cry upon its lips. Our Lord was at the point of death, breathing his last, when he cried *with a loud voice* and many tears: *Father, into thy hands I commend my spirit* (Lk 23:46). It was his last word; it was the supreme proof of the beloved Son's love for his Father.

When all else fails us, then, when we are at the end of our tether, that word, those dispositions, that surrender of our souls into the Savior's hands can never fail. The Son commended his spirit to the Father in his final unequaled death-throes; and we, when the turmoil of spiritual anguish deprives us of all relief, of all ability to hold out—we are to commend our spirits into the hands of this eternal Son, our true Father. Then, bowing our heads (cf. Jn 19:30) in compliance with his sweet will, we are to give our entire wills into his keeping.

(*Treatise* IX, 12)

We have a neat way of referring to death as a passing, and to the dead as the departed. It simply means that for human beings death is a passing from one life to another; to die is but to depart from the limitations of mortality and achieve immortality. The will can never die, any more than the soul; that is certain. Sometimes, however, it departs from the limits of its own natural life, to live entirely in the will of God. Then it neither knows nor cares what it wants; it surrenders itself utterly and unreservedly to the permissive will of providence, becoming so blended with this sweet will, so steeped in it, as to fade from view, *hidden away now with Christ in God* (Col 3:3), where it is alive to itself no longer, but God's will lives in it (cf. Gal 2:20).

What becomes of starlight when the sun appears on the horizon? It is not destroyed, to be sure; it is caught and absorbed into the sun's greater light. What becomes of the human will when it is completely surrendered to what God wants? It is not entirely lost, but so swallowed up in God's will, so blended with it, that there are no signs of it any longer, for it has no will other than God's.

After all, if you ask a servant in the retinue of some important person, where he is going, he ought not to reply by mentioning such or such a place, he should simply say that he is following his master. The servant, you see, does not go where *he* wants, but where his master wants to go.

In the same way people who defer to God's will should have no will of their own; they do only what God wants. A person on board ship is not travelling by his or her own motion, but by that of the ship; similarly, the heart embarked on doing what God wants should have no other desire but to be carried along by God's will. No longer do such persons say to God: *Only as thy will is, not as mine is* (Lk 22:42)—they have no ambitions of their own to give up. But they do say: "Lord, I commend my will into your hands (cf. Ps 30:6; Lk 23:46)"—as though indicating that their wills are no longer at their own disposal, but at the command of providence.

There is a difference here from masters and servants. A master plans his journey, his servant submits and follows; two people are involved, and so there are two wills. But if a person's will is dead to self, to come alive to God's will, it no longer chooses for itself, it not only complies with God's will and submits to it, it is utterly self-obliterated, transformed into the divine. That person is like a child in its mother's arms. The little one has not yet awakened to the awareness of a will of its own; it has no desire to be anywhere but in its mother's arms, believing itself to be one with her. It is not anxious about adapting itself to its mother's will; unaware that it has a will of its own, it leaves its mother to do and desire what she decides is best for it.

Most assuredly, the human will has reached the peak of perfection when it is united to the will of our supreme good as the psalmist's was, who said: *Thine to guide me with thy counsel* (Ps 72:24). All he meant was that he did not guide himself by his own counsel, by his own will, but left himself to be led and counseled by the will of God.

(*Treatise* IX, 13)

It is quite likely that the blessed Virgin, our Lady, found such happiness cradling her dear little Jesus in her arms that her contentment proved a barrier to weariness, or at least alleviated it. After all, if a branch of *Agnus Castus* eases and refreshes travelers, think of all the relief that glorious Mother experienced when carrying the spotless Lamb of God (cf. Jn 1:36; 1 Pt 1:19)! If she let him toddle beside her, holding him by the hand, it did not mean that she preferred this to feeling his arms around her neck; she was merely training him to walk by himself.

As for us, Theotimus, little children as we are of our Father in heaven, we can walk with him in two ways: First of all, we can walk on our own feet by using our own wills; we try to bring them into line with his, holding his hand by our obedience to his intention, by following wherever he leads us. This is what God demands of us through his declared will. He wants me to do what he enjoins, so he means me to have the will to do it. God has shown me that he wishes me to keep holy the day of rest. Since he means me to do so, he intends that I should determine to do it; to this end he means me to have a will of my own, to follow him by putting it in tune with his.

However, there is another way of walking with our Lord; when we have no will of our own, but simply allow ourselves to be carried in the arms of his permissive will by a wondrous consent which can be given the name of union—or rather, perfect oneness of will with God. You see, God's permissive will is nothing but the working out of his providence, events that happen beyond our control. Of course we can will them to happen in accord with God's will, and that is a good thing; but we can also, with perfect peace of soul, accept the events determined by providence—our wills unambitious, merely consenting to everything God means to do in us, for us, through us.

That is how we should be—tractable and docile to God's permissive will, as it were wax in his hands, never a desire or ambition of our own, but leaving God to will and provide for us as he pleases, throwing *back on him* (as St. Peter advises) *the burden of all our anxiety; he is concerned for us* (1 Pt 5:7). Notice that St. Peter says "all our anxiety"; in other words, both the things that happen to us and those we seek or avoid for ourselves. It will be his concern to bring everything right for us, to decide what is for the best.

Meanwhile, let us give ourselves over lovingly to praising God for all his benefits, after Job's example (cf. Jb 1:21): "Much the Lord has given me; he has also taken it away; blessed be the name of the Lord. Not a single event falls under my will, Lord, for I leave you to decide what happens to me just as you wish. Instead of deciding things for myself, I will praise your decisions." There you have our wills performing their highest function when they give up all effort at desiring or choosing for themselves the things that God's permissive will allows, to leave themselves free to praise and thank him for all he wills to happen.

(*Treatise* IX, 14)

To praise God, to thank him for all that his providence disposes, is a most pious practice—and no mistake. If, while we leave God to decide and do what he likes in, with and through us; if, while we pay no heed to what is happening, although we feel it keenly, we could distract ourselves, could concentrate on God's goodness and loving-kindness, praising it not only for what it disposes, but also for what it is in itself, its own excellence—we should obviously be doing something much holier still.

Once upon a time, a famous surgeon's daughter fell into a fever that lasted a long time. Aware of her father's deep affection for her, she remarked to one of her friends: "I am in great pain, but it never occurs to me to take any medicine; after all, I don't know what would be needed to cure me. I could want one thing, when I ought to have another. Isn't it better for me to leave all that to my father? He knows; he can also do and desire all that my health requires. It would be a mistake for me to think of doing anything; he is sufficiently concerned for me. It would be a mistake for me to decide on something; he will make the decisions that are best for me. I'm simply going to wait until he decides to do what he thinks fit; I shall merely look up at him when he comes to see me, to show him that I love and trust him."

With these words she fell asleep. Her father, however, deciding that she should be bled, made all the necessary preparations and then came to wake her up. After inquiring how she felt after her sleep, he asked if she would let herself be bled in order to get well.

"Father," she answered, "I am yours. I don't know what I should try, to cure myself; it is for you to decide and do whatever you think best. As for me, all I want is to love you with all my heart, as I do, and be a credit to you."

Well, they bound her arm, and her father himself set about opening the vein. As he made the incision and the blood spurted out, his daughter took no notice of the wound or the flow of blood, but kept her eyes fixed upon her father's face. No cry escaped her, but only now and then the gentle murmur: "My father loves me very much, and I am all his." When it was all over, she did not thank him; she merely repeated yet again her expressions of childlike love and trust.

Tell me now, Theotimus my friend, could this girl have shown a more considerate, a stronger love for her father, if she had pestered him with requests for something to cure her sickness, if she had watched him open the vein or gazed at the flow of blood, if she had been profuse in her thanks? There is not the slightest doubt about it. By thinking for herself, when her father was concerned for her, she would only have given herself useless worry; by watching her arm during the operation, she would merely have been frightened; by thanking her father, she would simply have been practicing one virtue—gratitude. Surely she did the best thing by concentrating on demonstrating her affection; this gave her father far greater pleasure than any single virtue could have done.

On the Lord I fix my eyes continually, trusting him to save my feet from the snare (Ps 24:15), from being caught in a trap. Has ill fortune ensnared you? Turn your attention from what has happened, from the trap into which you have fallen. Look up to God, leave matters to him; he will take care of you. *Cast the burden of thy cares upon the Lord, and he will sustain thee* (Ps 54:23; 1 Pt 5:7). Why become involved in the pros and cons of worldly events, of things that happen? You are ignorant of what you ought to wish for; God will make plans enough for you without the need for you to put yourself to the trouble. Await, your soul at peace, the outcome of God's permissive will. Be satisfied with what he wants; it is never anything but good. This was what he enjoined, after all, on his beloved Catherine of Siena: "Think of me," he told her, "and I shall take thought for you."

It is extremely difficult to put into words this complete self-surrender of the human will when it is thus consumed, when it is dead to everything but the will of God. We cannot say, in my opinion, that it complies with God's will, since compliance is an act by which the soul expresses consent; nor can we say that it accepts or welcomes God's will, inasmuch as these are what you might call passive activities by which we take and endure what happens to us; we cannot even say that it tolerates what God wants, since toleration is an act of the will—an idle form of willing, where we do not mean to do anything, but merely allow things to be done. So it seems to me that a person who is disinterested, who has no will of his or her own, but leaves God to decide as he pleases, should be simply said to keep the will on the alert, ready for anything. Anticipation is not constructive or active; it is merely holding oneself in readiness for something to happen. Such alertness of soul, remember, is clearly voluntary, yet it is not an action; it is simply a readiness to take what comes. Once events occur and are accepted, this anticipation is transformed into consent or compliance; before they happen, however, the soul in point of fact is simply on the alert, attentive, equally prepared for anything and everything that God's will disposes.

This is how the Savior's utter submission of his human will to the will
of his eternal Father is described in prophecy by Isaiah (cf. Is 50:5, 6). *An
attentive ear the Lord has given me;* in other words, he has made known
to me all the sufferings his permissive will has in store for me. And he
goes on to say: *Not mine to withstand him; not mine to shrink from the
task.* What does this mean except that his will was on the alert, held in
readiness for all that God should dispose? So he continues: *I offered my
body defenseless to the men who would smite me, my cheeks to all who
plucked at my beard,* prepared to let them have their way with me.

But notice, if you will, that the Savior was not satisfied with a prayer
of deference to his Father's will in the garden of Olives; he not only let
himself be taken, manhandled, pushed around by his executioners
through a wonderful surrender of his body and his life into their hands,
but he also placed his soul and his will—through a most perfect disinterestedness—in the hands of his eternal Father. Although he cried out: *My
God, my God, why hast thou forsaken me?* (Mt 27:46)—this was to bring
home to us the reality of the bitterness of his spiritual sufferings, and not
to run counter to his attitude of disinterested love. In fact he shortly made
this quite clear as he crowned life and passion with the matchless phrase:
Father, into thy hands I commend my spirit (Lk 23:46).

(*Treatise* IX, 15)

God's Will Strips . . . and Re-clothes

Let us picture to ourselves the gentle Jesus in Pilate's house. There,
for love of us, he was divested of his garments one by one at the hands
of soldiers, the agents of his death. Not content with that, they tore his
skin from him with cudgel-blows and whips. Later his soul was divested
of his body, his body bereft of life, by the death he suffered on the cross.
But in three days, through his holy resurrection, his soul re-assumed its
glorious body, while his body regained immortal flesh and clothed itself
in a variety of garbs—now a pilgrim, now a gardener—as humanity's
salvation and his Father's glory called for it.

All that was love's work, Theotimus. And it is also love at work when
a human soul is prompted to die happily to self and come alive to God; it
is love that divests it of all human desires, of all self-esteem—each as

close to spirit as skin to flesh—and lays it bare at last of even its darling emotions, such as fondness for spiritual consolations, practices of piety, perfection of virtue—all of which seemed to be the very life of a devoted soul.

Why then, the soul has good grounds for exclaiming: "*Ah, but my robe, I have laid it by: how can I put it on again? My feet,* my varied emotions, *I washed but now; shall I soil them afresh with the dust?* (Sg 5:3). *Naked I came, when I left* God's fashioning hand, *and whence I came, naked I must go.* Many ambitions *the Lord gave* me; now *the Lord has taken* them *away. Blessed be the name of the Lord* (Jb 1:21)." That same Lord who prompted us to desire virtues when we set out, who saw that we practiced them at every opportunity, now deprives us of any attachment to virtue or to spiritual exercises. He means us to grow in peace, purity, simplicity, so as to become impartial to all but God's sweet will.

Judith, the fair and chaste, kept many articles of finery in her wardrobe, yet she was not attached to them, nor ever wore them in her widowhood, except when God inspired her to be the undoing of Holofernes (cf. Jdt 10:3). So it should be with us: though we have learned to practice virtue, to perform our spiritual exercises, still we are not to become attached to them, not deck out our hearts in them, except we are aware that such is what God wants of us. Judith always wore mourning—but for this one occasion God meant her to appear in splendor; we too are to remain at peace in the garb of our wretchedness and weakness, until such time as God lends us the grace to do better things.

We cannot bear to remain naked long, stripped of all attachments. That is why St. Paul warns us (cf. Col 3:9, 10) that as soon as we are quit of the old self, and the habits that went with it, we must be re-clothed in the new self—that is, in Jesus Christ. When we have given up everything, even a fondness for virtue, so as to have no desire for this or for anything else but what God sees fit to send us, we are to clothe ourselves anew with other likings—perhaps even those we formerly renounced. We are to re-clothe ourselves in them, however, not for their attractiveness, their utility for us, not for the fact that they are creditable, fit to gratify our love for ourselves, but solely because God finds them attractive, because they redound to his honor, contribute to his glory.

If we have been divested of a previous attachment to spiritual consolations, to exercises of devotion, to the practice of virtue—yes, even to our growth in perfection—we are now to re-clothe ourselves with a

completely new tendency . . . which leads us to love God's graces and
blessings no longer as means to perfection, no longer as adornments of
the soul, but because our Lord's name is hallowed in them, his kingdom
advanced through them, his positive and permissive will glorified ty them
(cf. Mt 6:9, 10).

So it was that St. Peter put on his clothes in prison at the angel's
command, not of his own choice; on went belt, shoes and cloak (cf. Acts
12:8). Then there was St. Paul, stripped in an instant of all ambition: *Lord,*
he asked, *what wilt thou have me do* (Acts 9:6) In other words: "What
will you have me love now? By throwing me to the ground you have put
to death my self-will. Come, Lord, set your own sweet will in its place.
Thou art my God, teach me to do thy will (Ps 142:10)."

Theotimus, as a person who has given up everything for God, you
ought to take nothing back except as God wills: You will nourish your
body as God ordains, so that it may be servant to the spirit; you study now
with the sole idea of assisting your neighbor and your own soul as God
wants you to; you practice virtue, not insofar as they please you, but
insofar as God desires it.

God ordered Isaiah to strip himself naked (cf. Is 20:2, 3). This the
prophet did, and went about preaching like that for three whole days,
according to some commentators—three years, according to others. At
last, when the time prefixed by God expired, he put on his clothes again.
In the same way we are to strip ourselves of all attachments, little or great;
we are frequently to examine our consciences to see if we are ready, as
Isaiah was, to divest ourselves of all our garments. Then we too, when
the time comes, are to take up again such inclinations as are suited to
charity's service. Thus we shall be able to die naked with our Savior on
the cross, to rise again with him in newness of life (cf. Rom 6:4-6). *Not
death itself is so strong as love* (Sg 8:6) to make us release our hold on
everything; and charity is sublime as the resurrection to adorn us with
grandeur and glory.

(*Treatise* IX, 16)

Toward the Integration
of Life and Prayer

What Does it Mean to Love God Above All Things?

God demands this of us: of all our loves his must be the dearest, the supreme love of our hearts; it must be the deepest, filling our whole souls; it must be the most wholehearted, making use of all our faculties; and it must be the strongest, to which we give ourselves with might and main. Since it is a love by which we choose and set God upon the throne of our hearts, it is a love involving the highest choice, or a choice embracing the highest love.

As you know, Theotimus, there are several kinds of love—for example, parental, filial, sibling, conjugal; just as there is love of the company we keep, the people to whom we are indebted or on whom we depend. All these loves—and there are many more—differ in their perfection; each is so well adapted to its own purpose that it cannot be validly transferred to any of the others. The person who loves his or her father like a brother does not love him enough, that is certain; the man who only loves his wife as he does his father does not love her as he should.

Love resembles honor. Honors are distinguished by the variety of good qualities to which honor is due; in the same way loves are distinguished by the varied goodness which inspires them. The highest honor belongs to the highest perfection, and supreme love to the supreme goodness. Love of God is a love that knows no equal, for God's goodness is a goodness beyond compare. *Listen, then, Israel; there is no Lord but the Lord our God, and thou shalt love the Lord thy God with the love of thy whole heart, and thy whole soul,* and thy whole mind, *and thy whole strength* (Dt 6:4, 5). Since God alone is Lord, since his goodness is infinitely great, infinitely above all goodness, he must be loved with a love that makes us value so highly the blessing of being pleasing to him, that we prefer and care for God before all things else.

Surely you can see that people who love God in this way have devoted their whole soul and their whole strength to God. Always and for ever,

147

no matter what happens, they will prefer God's good grace to all things, ever ready to forgo the whole world to maintain their love for God.

(Treatise X, 6)

Of all our loves, God's is to be given such a place of honor that we are ever ready to give up all the others for love of him alone.

Sarah gave her maid-servant Hagar to her husband Abraham as his mate, in accord with the custom of those days, so that she might give him children; but once Hagar had conceived she greatly scorned her mistress. There was no way of telling up to then which of the two women Abraham loved the more, for Hagar shared his bed with Sarah and had the benefit of fertility. Only when these two loves conflicted did Abraham show where his deepest affection lay. No sooner had Sarah complained of being treated scornfully by Hagar that he replied: *Is she not in thy power, thy own maid-servant? Do what thou wilt with her* (Gn 16:6). This led Sarah to use Hagar so cruelly that she was forced to take refuge in flight. Charity means us to have other loves, and often we are unable to decide which is the heart's chief love. The human heart frequently shares its gratification with the love of creatures, so that its affection for created things is often much more active than its love for God. Yet charity does not fail to exceed all other loves—as events prove, when the creature stands in the way of the Creator. At such times we range ourselves on the side of charity; we submit to it all our other affections.

Sure enough, you will see a mother so busily engaged with her child that she would seem to have no love for anything else: her eyes see nothing but her baby, her lips serve only to kiss it, her breast is but to feed it, her only care is to rear it. You might think her husband meant nothing to her compared with her child. If she were faced with the choice of losing one or the other, however, it would be quite evident that she valued her husband more. Although her love for her baby is more tender, importunate, doting, her love for her husband is greater, stronger, deeper.

Therefore, when people love God for his infinite goodness, however little charity they may possess, they will prefer God's will to all things else. On every occasion that offers itself they will give up everything to keep themselves in God's grace; nothing could separate them from the supreme goodness. So that although charity is not as importunate or as touching as other loves, yet it is responsible at times for such noble and perfect actions that a single one of them is worth ten million of the others. Rabbits are incredibly prolific, while elephants never calve more than once; yet one baby elephant is of greater value than all the rabbits in the world. The love we have for created things is often extremely productive; charity's activity, however, is so supreme that it exceeds all others—it gives God the preference in everything without reserve.

(*Treatise* X, 7)

Is God's Love Tied to Personality Types?

Natural temperament plays no small part in the loving contemplation of God—wrote a great monk of this century—and people with affectionate natures have a distinct advantage. I do not think he means, however, that charity is apportioned to people or angels on the strength of natural qualities; nor does he mean that God shares his love with people in proportion to their natural traits and talents. This would contradict scripture; it would also infringe the Church's ruling denouncing the Pelagians as heretics.

All through this treatise I have been talking about the supernatural love which God, in his loving-kindness, pours out into our hearts. This love makes its home in the highest point of the soul, its very apex, independent of natural disposition. In one way, an affectionate nature temperamentally equips people for loving God; in another, it renders them liable to become too fond of created things. Such a natural tendency gives people an aptitude for loving God; it also makes it perilously possible for them to adulterate the purity of charity with a miscellany of other loves. Loving unworthily is the risk we run in loving easily.

It is true, however, that souls made in this way do wonderfully well in the love of God. Once they are purified from the love of creatures, charity finds it easy to permeate all their spiritual faculties. The result is a pleasing graciousness not apparent in those with bitter, peevish, gloomy or cross-grained temperaments.

But suppose there were two people equal in charity: one naturally kind and loving, the other of surly or sarcastic temperament. Undoubtedly they would both love God to the same extent, though not in the same way. The naturally kind-hearted person would love more easily, be more courteous, more gentle; but that love would not be stronger or more perfect. The love which springs from the obstacles and reluctance of a crabbed, unfeeling nature will be stronger, more illustrious; though the other may be more delightful and graceful.

A naturally affectionate disposition, therefore, counts for little when it comes to loving God, loving supernaturally. Theotimus, I would gladly tell everyone: "If your heart is inclined to love, why not aim at loving God? Even if you are not naturally affectionate, why not set your heart on supernatural love? God, from whom this holiest of invitations comes, will himself lovingly bestow it on you."

(Treatise XII, 1)

Is Love Hampered by Our Necessary Occupations?

Curiosity, ambition, anxiety, an unawareness or forgetfulness of why we are in this world—those are what fill our lives with many more difficulties than duties, much more worry than work, a great deal more bother than business. Foolish, empty, unnecessary pursuits which distract us from the love of God—these are the things that get in our way, not the genuine and proper duties of our state in life.

David, in the thick of danger or of duty, in peace or war, could always truthfully sing: *What else does heaven hold for me, but thyself? What charm for me has earth, here at thy side?* (Ps 72:25). Our own St. Louis too could say the same. Neither was St. Bernard's growth in charity retarded by days spent with the courts and armies of the great, playing the diplomat for the glory of God. A change of scene for him, but not a change of heart; a loving heart still, and a loyal one. As he might have put it: there were changes in his way of living, but his way of life remained unchanged; the work he had to do was different, but he was indifferent to the kind of work it was. No chameleon he; his environment worked no change upon his bearing: always united to God, he kept burnished the silver-gilt of his purity and his charity—shot, all the time, with humility.

I am well aware, Theotimus, of the wise men's warning:

From courtiers' ways and lawyers' pleas take flight.
Give God your service. Nor can soldiers' strife
Implant or cherish seeds of holy life:
'Tis peace that fathers faith and virtue bright.

And well might the Israelites, prisoners no less than strangers, decline to give the Babylonians a stave from the music sung at Sion:

O how could we sing
the song of the Lord
on alien soil?   (Ps 136:4)

A man who is a slave to courtly favors, legal triumphs, military honors—it is all over with him; he is no longer capable of the song of God's love. But God comes to the aid of the person who mixes in royal society, goes to war, or pleads at the bar only from a sense of duty; the pure air of heaven protects the heart from the plagues prevailing there.

During the plague in Milan, St. Charles never scrupled to visit houses or come in contact with infected people, when God's work called for it; but he would never have gone into danger, had there been no genuine necessity, for fear of tempting providence. No harm came to him for that reason. He was neither fainthearted nor foolhardy, merely trustful; so God's love kept him safe. God takes similar care of those whom duty calls to the court, the bar or the battlefield. No need, then, to be so timid as to omit something good, something lawful, by failing to respond; no call, either, to be so self-confident, so presumptuous as to engage in such things unless duty or rank leave no option.

(Treatise XII, 4)

Is Love Hampered by Lack of Great Opportunities?

The grandiose schemes some people evolve of doing great things for God! They dream of wonderful deeds, unusual sufferings—deeds and sufferings outside their present experience, and which will probably never come their way. This leads them to imagine that with one leap they have reached the heights of love. More often than not, it is just where they are wrong. They have simply let imagination grasp great crosses still in the far-distant future, while they zealously avoid burdening themselves with smaller ones around them in the present. That is the worst temptation of all: to be heroes in theory, cowards in practice.

God preserve us from fanciful fervor! Deep in our hearts it breeds the hidden germ of self-esteem. Important tasks lie seldom in our path; but all day long they are little things we can do so well, if we do them with all our love. That saint, with his glass of cold water for the thirsty traveler—little enough, it seems, his gesture; but so pure his intention, so perfect the kindness, the love, which he puts into what he is doing, that his simple offering becomes a spring of living water to bring him everlasting life (cf. Mt 10:42).

Bees pilfer from lily, iris, rose; but they take home as many spoils from smaller blooms of rosemary and thyme. Sweeter honey is the result, for nectar in tiny vessels is more concentrated, better preserved. Most assuredly, lowly minute deeds of devotion call not merely for a more frequent practice of charity, but normally for greater humility—so they are more worthwhile, productive of greater sanctity.

Fitting in with others' moods; putting up with boorish behavior; overcoming our own moods and passions; giving way over our own petty inclinations; trying to conquer our distaste for things and people; gladly recognizing our imperfections; struggling constantly to preserve our peace of soul; loving our humiliations; graciously accepting contempt amd criticism of our way of life, the company we keep, the things we do—all this does the soul more good, Theotimus, than we could ever dream, as long as God's love inspires it. But I have already explained this to Philothea.[1]

(Treatise XII, 6)

How to Bring Love to Everything One Does

Peacocks bred from birth in entirely white surroundings are said to be all white too. But this I know: if love for God informs our intentions, when we contemplate some good work or enter upon some profession, all our subsequent actions receive their value and derive their dignity from this love in which they originated. The natural activities of my profession—or

---

1.   *Introduction* III, 3

actions which are an essential part of what I have planned to do—obviously result from my original choice.

But we are not to be satisfied with that, Theotimus. Indeed, for any first-rate progress in devotion, it is not enough to form an initial or annual intention of living and working for God; we must make this offering every day—after the fashion of the morning exercise which I taught Philothea. This daily renewal puts the powerful imprint of love on all our actions, by re-directing our hearts to God's glory; thus it ever increases our holiness.

Let us, in addition, devote our lives to God's love over and over again throughout the day by means of ejaculatory prayer, spiritual aspirations, recollection. These pious practices—ever lifting our minds to God— bring our actions too in their train. Suppose a soul continually soars up toward God, incessantly forms acts of love to preserve union of heart with him—surely we can hold that God is the origin and motive of all the good which that soul does! Take a soul that says: "Thine I am (Ps 118:94), Lord; *all mine, my true love, and I all his* (Sg 2:16); my God and my all; my Jesus and my life—grant me the grace of dying to self, of coming alive to you! Oh, to love, to advance, to die to self, to live for God! Oh, to be so wrapped up in God that nothing else counts!" Surely the actions of such a soul are continually consecrated to the divine bridegroom. Blessed are those who have once achieved detachment (as I have previously explained[1]), who leave themselves entirely in God's hands; one sigh, one glance of theirs, will confirm their resolution of putting God first, of loving him in everything and everything for him.

This practice of continual aspirations is the best way of bringing love into everything we do—especially into the tiny, ordinary things of life. When it comes to unusual, important things, the following method (which I have already touched on elsewhere[2]) is the way to get the best results. Lift up heart and mind to God; concentrate on eternity. In the far reaches of eternity God's kindness cherished the idea of us; he planned everything that would help us to grow in his love and achieve salvation—especially the circumstances now offering us something good to be attempted or something evil to be endured. This done, we must open wide our arms to accept and welcome, with all the love we can muster, either the good that needs doing or the evil to be endured. In this way we please and obey God's providence, since from eternity he willed it all.

---

1. Book IX, chapter 16.
2. Book VIII, chapter 14.

That is the way to approach the hardest tasks, the worst sufferings life may bring. If they happen to be long drawn out, however, repeat the practice from time to time, as often as you can. This helps to keep your will united to the permissive will of God. *Be it so, Father,* you could say with our Lord, *since this finds favor in thy sight* (Mt 11:26). Heaven knows the treasures which this practice contains!

(*Treatise* XII, 9)

All for Jesus! Live Jesus!

And now, to end my book at last. . . . Our Lord's passion and death form the sweetest, strongest motive capable of quickening our hearts in this life. Samson found that bees had made a comb of honey in the lion he had slain; we shall find that the mystics achieved the perfection of charity in the wounds of *the Lion that comes from the tribe of Judah* (Rv 5:5), who was slain, broken and reviled on mount Calvary. Like Samson too the children of the cross are proud of their wonderful riddle, for which the world can find no meaning: out of death, eater of all things, comes the food of solace; out of death, strongest of all things, comes the honey of love (cf. Jgs 14:8, 14). Your death claims my love, Jesus my Savior, for it gave your love supreme expression.

In heaven too, next to the vision of God's essential goodness, our Savior's death will be the most potent source of rapture for the saints. This was revealed in the transfiguration, a foretaste of heaven, when *Moses and Elijah spoke* with our Lord *or the death which he was to achieve at Jerusalem* (Lk 9:31)—the death by which the world's lover was robbed of life, to give it to those he loved. And I can imagine the incessant repetition of this paean in the eternal song of heaven:

All for Jesus! In whose latest breath
Love was stronger still than death.

Calvary is the mount of lovers. Love which does not spring from the Savior's passion is a perilous plaything. Heaven help the deathbed devoid of Christ's love; and heaven help that love which has no reference to Christ's death! In our Lord's passion love and death blend so inextricably, no heart can contain one without the other. No life, without love, on

Calvary; no love without the Redeemer's death. Beyond that, only two ways lie open—eternal death or eternal love; and the essence of Christian wisdom lies in making the right choice. To help you there, Theotimus, I have written this book.

> One path alone our feet must tread
> While this life lasts, and God holds sway:
> Eternal love, or death—the choice;
> And God has left no middle way.

Eternal love—my soul demands it; my choice is made! Yes, "come Holy Spirit, fill the hearts of your faithful and kindle in them the fire of your love."[1] Love or death! Death *and* love! Death to all other loves, to live for love of Jesus, to escape eternal death. Why, living in your eternal love, Savior of our souls, let this be our song for ever: "All for Jesus![2] I love Jesus! All for Jesus, my love! I love Jesus living and reigning for ever and ever. Amen."

And so I bring this long treatise to a close in words which echo St. Augustine's—when, before an eminent congregation, he concluded a wonderful sermon on charity: Charity inspired and penned these pages for you, dear Theotimus. May their contents find a lasting place in your heart, where charity can practice, rather than praise, my preaching. So be it. Blessed be God!

(Treatise XII, 13)

---

1. Cf. Mass of Pentecost.
2. *Vive Jésus*, which became the motto of the Visitation of Holy Mary, and which is usually translated, "Live Jesus!" See *Francis de Sales, Jane de Chantal, Letters of Spiritual Direction*, p. 9 *et passim*.

Chronology

1567   Born on August 21 at the Chateau de Sales near Thorens in the Duchy of Savoy, the first-born of François de Boisy and Françoise de Sionnaz. Baptized Francis Bonaventure in the parish church of St. Maurice in Thorens.

1573   Early education began at La Roche-sur-Foron and then at the College Chappuisien in Annecy.

1578   Began a ten-year stay in Paris, attending the Jesuit College of Clermont, studying the humanities and philosophy, and theology on his own initiative.

1586   December; beginning of an emotional and spiritual crisis, which was to last six weeks.

1588   After a brief visit to Savoy, left for the University of Padua to study law.

1590   The crisis of Paris resurfaced on a more theological level.

1591   September; received doctorate in civil and canon law.

1592   Admitted to the bar at the Senate of Savoy, Chambery.

1593   Named Provost of the cathedral chapter of Geneva on March 7; ordained priest on December 18 at the cathedral in Annecy.

1594   Beginning of the four-year mission to the Chablais region, south of Lake Geneva.

1597   Three secret meetings in Geneva with Théodore de Bèze.

1599   Called to Rome by Pope Clement VIII and appointed coadjutor to the bishop of Geneva.

1600   Publication of his *Defense of the Standard of the Cross.*

1601   Death of his father at age 79.

1602   January to September; second stay in Paris on religious and diplomatic missions. Frequents the Acarie spiritual circle, preaches in many Paris churches.

1602   En route back to Annecy Francis learned of his predecessor's death; was ordained bishop of Geneva, December 8, in the church of his baptism.

1604   Preached the Lenten series in Dijon; first meeting with Jane Frances Fremyot, Baroness de Chantal. In August they met at St. Claude, and he agreed to be her spiritual director.

1606   Established, together with Antoine Favre, the Florimontane Academy in Annecy.

1607 Second visit of Jane de Chantal to Sales; Francis shared with her his idea for a new form of religious life.
      Francis began writing a "life of holy charity" which would become his *Treatise on the Love of God.*

1608 Francis completed the first edition of the *Introduction to the Devout Life.*

1610 Death of his mother, Madame de Boisy, at age 58.
      Foundation, with Jane de Chantal, of the Visitation of Holy Mary in Annecy.

1616 *Treatise on the Love of God* published in Lyons.

1618 November 1618 to September 1619, final visit to Paris; contacts with Angélique Arnauld, Vincent de Paul, *et al.*

1619 Publication of the definitive edition of the *Introduction to the Devout Life.*

1622 Francis died while in Lyons, age 55.

1623 Transfer of his body from Lyons to the Visitation chapel in Annecy, arriving there January 24.

1661 Beatified by Pope Alexander VII.

1665 Canonized by the same on April 19.

1854 Declared Patron of the Deaf by Pope Pius IX.

1877 Declared a Doctor of the Church by the same.

1923 Declared Patron of Catholic Journalists and of the Catholic Press by Pope Pius XI.

Select Bibliography

Some Works of Francis de Sales in Translation

Introduction to the Devout Life. Translated by Armind Nazareth, Antony Mookenthottam and Antony Kolencherry. Bangalore, India: SFS Publications, 1990.

_____. Translated by John K. Ryan. New York: Doubleday, 1989.

_____. Translated by Michael Day. "Everyman's Library." New York: Dutton, 1961.

Introduction to the Devout Life, a Popular Abridgment. Abridged by Yvonne Stephan. Translated by Joseph D. Bowler and Lewis S. Fiorelli. Rockford, Ill.: Tan Books and Publishers, 1990.

The Love of God, a Treatise. Translated by Vincent Kerns. Westminster, Md.: Newman Press, 1962.

Treatise on the Love of God. 2 vols. Translated by John K. Ryan. Rockford, Ill.: Tan Books and Publishers, 1974.

Francis de Sales, Jane de Chantal, Letters of Spiritual Direction. Translated by Péronne Marie Thibert, selected and introduced by Wendy M. Wright and Joseph F. Power. "Classics of Western Spirituality." New York: Paulist Press, 1988.

St. Francis de Sales, Selected Letters. Translated by Elisabeth Stopp. New York: Harper and Bros., 1960.

The Sermons of St. Francis de Sales. Translated by Nuns of the Visitation, edited by Lewis S. Fiorelli. Rockford, Ill: Tan Books and Publishers, 1985—. Vol. 1: *On Prayer*. Vol. 2: *On Our Lady*. Vol. 3: *Lent*. Vol. 4: *Advent and Christmas*.

Works about Francis de Sales

Bedoyere, Michael de la. *François de Sales*. New York: Harper, 1960.

Henry-Couannier, Maurice. *Saint Francis de Sales and His Friends*. Translated by Veronica Morrow. Staten Island, N.Y.: Alba House, 1960.

Muller, Michael. *St. Francis de Sales*. New York: Sheed and Ward, 1937; reprint, Bangalore, India: SFS Publications, 1984.

Ravier, André. *Francis de Sales, Sage and Saint*. Translated by Joseph D. Bowler. San Francisco: Ignatius Press, 1988.

Wright, Wendy M. *Bond of Perfection: Jeanne de Chantal and François de Sales*. New York: Paulist Press, 1985.